BREAK FREE FROM INTRUSIVE THOUGHTS

BREAK FREE FROM INTRUSIVE THOUGHTS

An Evidence-Based Guide for Managing Fear and Finding Peace

DEBRA KISSEN, PhD, MHSA
MICAH IOFFE, PhD
EMILY LAMBERT, LPC, NCC

ROCKRIDGE
PRESS

Interior and Cover Designer: Amanda Kirk
Art Producer: Sue Bischofberger
Editor: John Makowski
Production Editor: Andrew Yackira

Cover photography © Beautiful landscape/shutterstock.com

Debra Kissen's author photo courtesy of Edyta Grazman Photography.
Micah Ioffe's author photo courtesy of Martha Schickler Photography.

ISBN: Print 978-1-64876-603-9 | eBook 978-1-64739-886-6

R0

Contents

This book is dedicated to all of our wonderful clients—who came to us terrified of their intrusive thoughts and through their hard, important work, soon reclaimed their lives and no longer felt held hostage by their anxiety.

Introduction and How to Use This Book

Humans all have intrusive thoughts. In fact, they are so common that 94 percent of people report having experienced intrusive thoughts at some point in their lives (Moulding et al., 2014). The main difference between those who struggle with intrusive thoughts and others who barely notice when these strange thoughts surface is how they relate to these brain invaders.

Some people immediately identify these thoughts as "spam mail" for the brain, while others—including you, if you are struggling with intrusive thoughts—view them as priority mail, carrying critical information about your intentions and overall character. This book's mission is to help you develop a new relationship with your intrusive thoughts. By reading this book and engaging in the recommended strategies, your brain will come to understand that intrusive thoughts are "all bark and no bite," and cannot harm you.

Part 1 of this book will give you a solid understanding of why you experience intrusive thoughts, what these thoughts mean and don't mean about you, and when these thoughts become clinically relevant. We will also provide you with an overview of the gold standard in treatment for intrusive thoughts. Part 2 of this book contains evidence-based tools and techniques to help you do the work of moving through, and soon beyond, your intrusive thoughts.

We can't promise you will never again experience an intrusive thought after you finish this book, but we are confident you will experience much less of the distress, anxiety, and impaired functioning caused by this mental noise. This work is not easy, but the journey is powerful and transformative.

You'll soon live your life with a greater sense of peace and satisfaction.

Before we get to work, we the authors wanted to take a few moments to introduce ourselves to you. We are three anxiety specialists who work together at Light on Anxiety CBT Treatment Center, where we offer therapy for anxiety and related behavioral health conditions. We use treatment protocols that are supported by data and research to help many people just like you to move past intrusive thoughts and get back to their lives. After working with so many wonderful clients, we decided to make our experience and knowledge base accessible to a broader audience by writing a brief blog post on obtaining freedom from intrusive thoughts. We were thrilled to see how that little bit of education and support became so impactful. Many readers reached out to tell us that they no longer felt alone nor felt that there was something wrong with them. We realized that if one blog post could provide so much healing, we could only imagine how much hope and peace a book filled with tips and tools could provide to those struggling with intrusive thoughts.

We are honored to serve as your guides and cheering section as you move from prisoner to dispassionate observer of your intrusive thoughts.

With much respect & appreciation,
Debra Kissen, PhD, MHSA
Micah Ioffe, PhD
Emily Lambert, LPC, NCC

PART ONE

WHAT YOU NEED TO KNOW ABOUT INTRUSIVE THOUGHTS

The first section of this book will provide you with the why, what, and when of intrusive thoughts. You'll learn why humans experience these thoughts, and what they mean and don't mean about you. You will also learn about the evidence-based treatment protocol that targets your intrusive thoughts to help you break free from them.

CHAPTER ONE

What Are Intrusive Thoughts?

THIS CHAPTER IS YOUR INTRUSIVE THOUGHT 101 introductory class. You will learn what causes intrusive thoughts, what experiencing them means about you, and perhaps more importantly, what they do not mean about you. You'll also learn how to see these thoughts for what they really are, rather than what they claim to be.

Defining Intrusive Thoughts

We've all had a strange thought or image pop into our head, seemingly out of the blue, from time to time. You may have been sitting in a crowded house of worship and during a moment of silent meditation, had an image surface of you standing up and yelling out inappropriate utterances. Or maybe as you slowed down at a stop sign and waited for a family with young children to pass, you had the thought, *What if I remove my foot from the brake and instead slam the accelerator?* These are both common examples of intrusive thoughts.

As the term suggests, intrusive thoughts surface out of the blue, intrude upon your ongoing thought process, and startle you with their attention-grabbing content or imagery. For example, if you are sitting at your desk paying bills and suddenly have the thought, *What if I grab the letter opener and stab myself in the eyeball?*, this would be considered an intrusive thought. This mental experience has all of the markings of an intrusive thought. It includes an aggressive quality and punctures your current moment with an impatient, petulant demand for your immediate attention above all else. In contrast, if you are sitting at your desk paying bills and suddenly have the thought, *What am I going to eat for lunch today?*, this would not be considered an intrusive thought because it lacks the jarring, dangerous quality of a thought that demands to be immediately attended to.

An additional noteworthy quality of intrusive thoughts is their *ego-dystonic* nature, meaning they express wishes or desires that oppose your values and beliefs. An *ego-syntonic* thought, on the other hand, matches with your values and beliefs. If a new mom who cherishes her newborn has the thought, *I will do everything in my power to protect my child and help her live her life to the fullest*, this is considered an ego-syntonic thought. If this same mom has the thought,

What if I stick my baby in the garbage can when I take out the trash?, this would be considered an ego-dystonic thought.

WHY DO PEOPLE HAVE INTRUSIVE THOUGHTS?
The goal of an intrusive thought is to startle you into paying attention to the worst dangers imaginable, and to prevent that catastrophic event from occurring. These thoughts highlight potential calamities of such extreme proportions that if they actually happened, life would potentially no longer be worth living.

Sometimes intrusive thoughts can be helpful. Imagine you are driving your family on a road trip and you fall asleep at the wheel. A useful intrusive thought would be: *Wake up! Your family is in immediate danger!* If you are boiling water and your toddler crawls by the stove as the pot bubbles over, a helpful intrusive thought would be: *Grab the baby now!* But other times, intrusive thoughts simply point out outlandish potential dangers that are unlikely to occur.

What's the Flip Side of Your Intrusive Thoughts?

Generating intrusive thoughts requires so much energy that your brain won't waste time creating them on topics of little importance. You will never have an intrusive thought like, *What if I lose control and drink a glass of water?* Instead, intrusive thoughts tend to encircle that which is most important to you and what makes life worth living for you.

For example, the teachers we work with, who enter their line of work because they love children, often have intrusive thoughts about engaging in inappropriate behaviors with their students. Parents may have intrusive thoughts about harming their newborn child. Newlyweds may experience intrusive thoughts about engaging in sexually inappropriate behaviors with people other than their partners.

If these individuals did not care about those most important to them, they would not be having these particular thoughts. The next time you are experiencing an intrusive thought, try to determine what core value and aspect of your life this thought is ineffectively attempting to protect.

Experiencing intrusive thoughts can be emotionally painful and uncomfortable, so you may as well make some lemonade out of intrusive thought (IT) lemons and gain some valuable insight from the discomfort. We recommend taking a bit of time to reflect on and clarify your values, as revealed by your intrusive thoughts.

WHEN DO INTRUSIVE THOUGHTS BECOME PROBLEMS?

Intrusive thoughts are a normal part of life. As mentioned in the introduction, research from 16 universities worldwide found that 94 percent of people experience intrusive thoughts at some point in their lives. In contrast, the National Institute of Mental Health indicates that 1 percent of the population will experience clinically significant stress and anxiety associated with their intrusive thoughts.

If you are reading this book, chances are good that you or a loved one falls into that 1 percent, and you have a difficult time moving past these thoughts. You may frequently find yourself (or others) vacillating between compulsively reviewing these thoughts to determine what they mean about you or desperately attempting to escape from and avoid them at all costs.

If you are experiencing emotional distress related to intrusive thoughts and assigning meaning to the experience of having a strange, disturbing thought intruder, then you are caught in a thinking trap known as *thought-action fusion*. Thought-action fusion is the belief that having a thought is equivalent to engaging in a behavior, and that having a "bad thought" means you are a "bad person." Thought-action fusion entails putting your thoughts on a pedestal and acting as if they mean something about you, your desires, and your worth. This book will help you to shift from a state of thought-action fusion, where thoughts feel equivalent to behaviors, to an understanding of thoughts as nothing more than electrical signals being transmitted within your brain.

Types of Intrusive Thoughts

If you are struggling with intrusive thoughts and experiencing emotional discomfort and life impairment associated with them, it is likely you hold the inaccurate belief that these thoughts reflect your true urges and desires. Prior to learning and deeply grasping the true essence of intrusive thoughts (hint: "brain spam") it is common to fear being judged as "disturbed" or "sick" or "evil" if an external party learned of the content and imagery of these thoughts.

When we begin working with a new client who is looking to get unstuck from their intrusive thoughts, we always first review a list of the top 10 most common intrusive thoughts before having the client share their own.

THE TOP 10 MOST COMMON INTRUSIVE THOUGHTS (ITs)

1. **Sexual Act ITs, for example:**
   - Having the thought, urge, or image of engaging in a sexually inappropriate behavior, such as an image of touching your dog's butt
   - Having the thought, urge, or image of sexually assaulting someone, such as the image of touching someone sexually despite their protests

2. **Sexual and Gender Identity ITs, for example:**
   - Having the thought, urge, or image of being attracted to the same sex (if someone self-identifies as being heterosexual) or having the thought, urge, or image of being attracted to the opposite sex (if someone self-identifies as being gay)

Having the thought, urge, or image of being transgender (if someone self-identifies as being cisgendered)

3. **Pedophilia ITs, for example:**
   - Having the thought, urge, or image of staring at a child's "private parts"
   - Having the thought, urge, or image of being turned on due to an interaction with a child

4. **Blasphemous ITs, for example:**
   - Having the thought, urge, or image of something related to being "anti-God" or "pro-Devil," such as having the thought *I love Satan*
   - Having the thought, urge, or image of engaging in a sexual act with a current or historical religious figure, such as the image surfacing of engaging in a sexual act with a statue of the Virgin Mary

5. **Harm/Violence ITs, for example:**
   - Having the thought, urge, or image of violently attacking an external party (most often someone who your mind considers weak or vulnerable such as a child, an elderly person, or a loved one in their sleep)
   - Having the thought, urge, or image of losing control and stabbing a loved one in your sleep

6. **Harming Children ITs, for example:**
   - Having the thought, urge, or image of violently attacking a child
   - Having the thought, urge, or image of losing control, emotionally and psychologically traumatizing a child due to your inappropriate emotional display

7. **Personal Safety ITs, for example:**
   - Having the thought, urge, or image of losing control and jumping out a window or off a balcony or any other high ledge
   - Having the thought, urge, or image of losing control and stabbing yourself with a knife

8. **Grotesque ITs, for example:**
   - Having the thought, urge, or image of mangled, bloody body parts
   - Having the thought, urge, or image of rotting flesh, with maggots crawling about

9. **Socially Transgressive ITs, for example:**
   - Having the thought, urge, or image of standing up and screaming when attending a crowded event where silence is the social expectation, such as when seeing a play or attending a religious event
   - Having the thought, urge, or image of tearing off clothing and running around naked

10. **Doubt ITs, for example:**
   - Having the thought, urge, or image of engaging in inappropriate behavior while sleeping or intoxicated and therefore being unable to prove to yourself with 100 percent certainty that it did not occur
   - Having the thought, urge, or image of engaging in an inappropriate behavior years ago that perhaps you repressed and is now beginning to surface

Highlighting for our clients that these strange, disturbing intrusive thoughts are actually quite common is one of the most rewarding aspects of our work. We review this top 10 list with clients in the initial phase of obtaining treatment for intrusive thoughts, then enjoy sitting back and noting the instant tension release they inevitably experience.

No Matter the Category, There's Help

Effective treatment for intrusive thoughts entails learning to see what these thoughts truly are, then learning to play with them instead of running away.

Imagine a young child who fears there is a monster living under their bed. One day they get the nerve to look and see if it is really there. Picture the freedom this child would feel when exploration uncovers dust bunnies but no monsters. This book will provide you with tools and techniques to help you face your intrusive thoughts head-on and extinguish them of their shock value. You will then be free to live life on your own terms—your intrusive thoughts no longer dictating what you should or should not do.

Meet Some Fellow Travelers

To assist you in gaining freedom from intrusive thoughts and decreasing the pain and suffering associated with them, you'll meet a few of the wonderful clients we have had the honor of working with. (Anonymously, of course, with key identifying information altered.) You will continue to get to know them throughout this book, as we journey through—and soon past—their intrusive thoughts, and yours.

"Tanisha," a 33-year-old woman who teaches math and science in a second-grade classroom, and volunteers once a week as a math tutor for middle schoolers from low-income neighborhoods.

"Greg," a 47-year-old man who works as a lawyer during the day and spends much of his free time in the evenings and on weekends with his wife and children.

"Lucas," a 38-year-old man successfully beginning his own start-up in the restaurant industry.

"Chloe," a 24-year-old woman who recently graduated from college at the top of her class and started her dream job in public relations for an environmental nonprofit.

Exercise: Match the intrusive thoughts (a to g) to the client who you think is most likely to have had this concern.

a. *I'm going to stab my wife and children.*
b. *I'm going to wake up one night, smothering my wife with a pillow.*
c. *I'm a pedophile.*
d. *How can I be sure I've never had sex with a child? What if I just don't remember?*
e. *I'm going to suddenly start swearing during a board meeting.*
f. *I'm going to use a racial slur the next time I talk with an African American colleague.*
g. *I'm going to go crazy on the subway to work, and they'll have to stop the train to calm me down and everyone will realize I've lost my mind.*

Answers: Tanisha: c, d; Greg: a, b; Lucas: g; Chloe: e, f

Key takeaway: Experiencing a scary, intrusive thought is not the same thing as engaging in a scary behavior. Those struggling with intrusive thoughts are not amoral "monsters." They are simply regular people who are extremely intolerant of having bad thoughts, and soon find themselves working so hard not to have certain thoughts that they end up increasing the frequency of the thoughts they are trying so hard to avoid.

Obtaining the Appropriate Level of Assistance

It is helpful to fill out a pre-intervention assessment to quantify the frequency and intensity of your symptoms, as you begin the work of freeing yourself from your intrusive thoughts.

1. In the past week, on average, how much emotional distress did you experience when an intrusive thought surfaced (using a 0 to 10 scale, with 0 being none and 10 being a lot)?

2. In the past week, on average, how much did the experience of intrusive thoughts affect your ability to engage effectively in your life and tend to all of your important life responsibilities (using a 0 to 10 scale, with 0 being none and 10 being a lot)?

3. How much effort and energy are you spending trying to resist or avoid intrusive thoughts (using a 0 to 10 scale, with 0 being none and 10 being a lot)?

This book is an appropriate first step if you are experiencing mild to moderate distress and discomfort, and your average answer to the assessment questions is 5 or below.

If you are experiencing severe impairment and your average answer to the assessment questions is 6 or above, you may find it helpful to obtain some outside assistance to help you gain freedom from intrusive thoughts. In addition, if you are having thoughts about hurting yourself or someone else, and if you have started to make plans to enact any of these behaviors, it is important to obtain mental health treatment to assist you in proceeding forward in your life. For crisis support, please see the Resources section on page 140 to get immediate help. If this is happening, it doesn't make you a bad person. It's not shameful, but it's hard to live with, and deserves professional attention. Also, if you are drinking or using drugs (including abusing prescription medications) in order to self-medicate or lower your anxiety, you deserve assistance to decrease your reliance on external substances so you can increase your contact with your internal power and strength.

Keep in mind that getting help is not a sign of weakness or failure. Far from it! We firmly believe that *everyone* could benefit from therapy at some point in their life—we have all received it!—and that being able to recognize those points is a skill that will make your life much easier. When symptoms reach a moderate to severe level, recovery will progress faster with the help of a trained professional.

Getting help for intrusive thoughts as well as other mental health concerns is easier than you would think. You can simply speak with your primary care physician and let them know you are looking for help to work on intrusive thoughts. You can even bring this book to help further explain the challenges you are experiencing.

We are sharing a lot of information with you about the experiences of intrusive thoughts, and you may be feeling overwhelmed as you attempt to process this information. We recommend checking in with yourself and paying attention to your anxiety level every few pages. If your anxiety level is 7 or above, chances are your brain and body are too busy being stressed and anxious to fully grasp the material we are sharing with you. Instead we recommend taking a break from reading and engaging in a physical activity, like taking a walk or doing jumping jacks—anything that allows you to release some of the excess energy you are storing. Please do come back to the book after this small break, as freedom from intrusive thoughts awaits you with each new concept you learn and technique you practice.

CHAPTER TWO

How Intrusive Thoughts Work

AS DISCUSSED IN CHAPTER 1, INTRUSIVE THOUGHTS are a normal part of the human experience. If you are experiencing intrusive thoughts, congratulations! You've received confirmation that you are human. Although these intrusive thoughts bring up a lot of discomfort and *feel* all-so-powerful, the power is actually not within the thoughts themselves. It is your reaction to these thoughts that powers a relentless cycle of anxiety and emotional pain.

The Cycle of Intrusive Thoughts

When you are experiencing an uncomfortable situation in other aspects of your life, what do you do? You could actively do something to make it go away, or you could avoid it and not be around it. These are both appropriate reactions to unwanted experiences.

These reasonable strategies unfortunately backfire when it comes to intrusive thoughts. When you react to a disturbing thought by trying to make it go away, this actually causes the thought to appear more frequently. Similarly, when you avoid a disturbing thought because it feels too painful to bear, this also makes the thought appear more often. The more you fight with these thoughts, the more ITs you will experience.

You are probably all too familiar with the cycle of intrusive thoughts. First, an IT or image pops into your head. Next, your brain believes the thought is true, and creates meaning about your intentions, or you as a person. Your anxiety then understandably spikes. Sitting with these thoughts feels really uncomfortable, so your brain naturally hops into protection mode and decides to react by either desperately trying to make them go away or to avoid them. This reaction is called a *compulsion* or a *safety behavior*—any behavior that attempts to get rid of your anxious feelings and can sometimes result in a short period of relief.

But as soon as the relief fades and the unwanted thoughts reappear, your brain remembers that all you need to do to feel that relief again is to react to or avoid your intrusive thoughts, restarting the painful cycle of ITs. The problem with engaging in a compulsion or safety behavior is that your brain never has the opportunity to learn relief is possible by simply letting these thoughts pass on their own. You really don't have to do anything at all to feel that relief, except ride the wave of anxiety. And each time you do this, you build up distress tolerance skills to help make that wave a little more tolerable.

REACTING: WHATEVER YOU DO, MAKE IT GO AWAY

It is common for those struggling with intrusive thoughts to engage in a set of mental and/or physical behaviors, or compulsions or safety behaviors, in an attempt to make the bothersome thoughts "go away" or to neutralize them.

Common examples of compulsions associated with intrusive thoughts are:

- Trying to "figure out" why you are having the intrusive thought and what it means about you.
- Checking arousal level and other physical sensations around feared people to determine if your intrusive thoughts represent your true feelings and desires.
- Repetitively googling to learn more about a phenomenon, to determine how similar or different you are from people who have demonstrated these frightening, aggressive, or offensive behaviors.

- Mentally reviewing to determine if you engaged in a feared behavior in the past or if you have the potential or desire to engage in a feared behavior in the future.
- Wearing certain clothes or engaging in tasks a certain way to feel safe, in control, or "just right."
- Seeking reassurance from others to obtain external feedback that you would never engage in a feared behavior and that you are in fact a "good person."
- Confessing to friends and loved ones that you are having a disturbing thought as a way of relieving guilt and checking to see that they still consider you a decent person.

AVOIDING: WHATEVER YOU DO, DON'T THINK

One of the first and most logical strategies that people try when experiencing uncomfortable, frightening intrusive thoughts is distraction. It is common to scroll through social media, watch TV, search the web, or do just about anything as long as it does not involve thinking.

Unfortunately, it is impossible to outmaneuver your own mind, no matter how hard you try. As we are sure you have experienced, wherever you go, your mind is right there beside you, chattering away about all of the things you would prefer not to think about. We humans just aren't very good at "not thinking" about things. The more we try to not think about an intrusive thought or any other topic, the more we find ourselves thinking about it. The thought becomes stuck.

This phenomenon occurs because the only way to know if we are successfully not thinking about a topic is to scan our minds for that content. Scanning our minds for an unwanted thought triggers it, so when we tell our brains not to think about that thought, we are actually thinking about that thought.

RUMINATING: WHATEVER YOU DO, THINK MORE

Rumination involves repetitive and extensive focus on all the negative aspects of a situation. It may involve thoughts about the past, thinking about all the times you did or said something a certain way. It could also focus on the future, thinking about what you may do or say in hypothetical situations. You may feel that if you are able to think through all the ways things went wrong, then you can be prepared for anything that could go terribly wrong in the future.

Ruminating is a reaction that feeds into worsening your anxiety and fueling the intrusive thought cycle, adding even more doses of belief and meaning into the thoughts. When you are in actual danger, one way your brain tries to help you to safety is to go into problem-solving mode—brainstorming and using all your creative juices to react to the challenge in front of you. While this reaction can be super helpful in situations of real danger, you may have experienced that it can be physically and emotionally exhausting if you are not actually in danger, but your brain buys into the intrusive thought's misinformation and believes you are.

YOUR INNER DIALOGUE

We all have conversations with ourselves, whether it's coaching ourselves through a future situation or deciding what we want to eat for breakfast. While at times they may feel silly, these inner dialogues are key to shaping our mood and actions. Our brains fall into certain types of thought patterns and internal dialogues that either help to manage or exacerbate anxiety. How you respond to intrusive thoughts plays an important role in managing your discomfort.

When you are tuned in to your internal dialogue, it feels like your thoughts are true, valid, and justified, and that you need to react to unwanted and disturbing thoughts. Noticing and observing your internal dialogue can help you become more aware of your intrusive thought cycles. The more you know about your inner dialogue, the more you can "catch" your reactions to intrusive thoughts and do something different.

THE ROLE OF UNCERTAINTY

Uncertainty can feel uncomfortable, unsettling, and unpredictable. Our brains naturally want to avoid uncertainty, because, logically, if we know how things will be, we can stay safe. Yet, uncertainty is the only thing in life we can truly be certain about. So now what?

Living with uncertainty is challenging and doable. The challenge is that your brain wants to know for certain that you aren't a bad person or that you won't actually say or do anything that feels wrong. Naturally, you are probably willing to do just about anything you can to gain that certainty. Instead, this book and an intrusive thought treatment approach will teach you how to lean into not knowing for sure what may happen. If that feels like an impossible task right now, that is okay. Uncertainty can feel scary, but we are here to guide you through it and to help you rewire your brain to tolerate and learn to embrace it.

HOW A THOUGHT BECOMES A PROBLEM

As discussed, intrusive thoughts are not the problem. They become a problem when you become consumed with trying to not to have these thoughts and in the process get stuck in a battle with them.

Think about the first time you "met" your very first intrusive thought. Your first reaction to it may have been confusion. It may have been very bothersome or shocking. As you have now learned, this was the first part of your intrusive thought cycle. Your anxiety alarm bells sounded, and then all you could think of was this unwanted thought. Then you tried to harness that desired certainty and do what you could to stop the thought. Finally, your intrusive thought became stuck, taking up all your precious mental space and energy.

The Brain

Your wonderfully complex brain is made up of hundreds of billions of interconnected neurons that enable it to communicate between different brain structures. Intrusive thoughts originate from your *Prefrontal Cortex* (PFC), a region within the frontal lobes of your brain. The PFC is responsible for logical thinking and reasoning, planning, organizing, and other important higher-order cognitive processes. It manages all types of thoughts, including unwanted ones. And when an intrusive thought pops up in your PFC, your anxiety response is triggered through connections to your amygdala, the part of your brain that is on high alert for danger in your surroundings.

It's important to know that it is possible to rewire these connections in your brain to operate more effectively and in a way that works for you. Neuroplasticity means that your brain can change over time and adapt to new experiences. Rewiring these neural connections to learn something new or think about things differently can be strengthened with repetition and time. This book will assist you in rewiring your brain to move through and past intrusive thoughts.

The Truth about Intrusive Thoughts

Think about a time when you had the hiccups. Did it startle you? Did you think they would last forever? How much time did you spend trying to stop them? And what about when you stopped hiccupping? Can you remember your last hiccup? Probably not, because you likely shifted your focus to something more important to you, and eventually this repetitive bodily function ran its annoying course.

We like to think about intrusive thoughts as brain hiccups: a part of the human experience, not worth being alarmed by, not signaling anything wrong with your body or health, and something that comes and goes as you move about your life. In the following sections, you'll learn about how to accurately think about your intrusive thoughts and debunk some myths that only make you feel stuck.

THOUGHTS ARE JUST THOUGHTS, AND NOT ALL THOUGHTS ARE IMPORTANT

Thoughts come in all shapes and sizes. We have thoughts that help us take action about things that are important to us (such as, *I need to walk the dog*) and we have thoughts that keep us stuck and feeling uncomfortable (such as, *I hope I don't stab my partner in my sleep*, which usually is not an imminent danger). A thought that repeats or grows with intensity is *not* a signal of its importance. Remember, like a hiccup that is not an important indicator of health, intrusive thoughts are not indicators of anything important or threatening.

EVERYONE HAS INTRUSIVE THOUGHTS

The PFC churns out thoughts rapidly in all of our brains, to help improve our functioning and to help us interact with the world around us. However, we are on a spectrum of how intense, loud, and intrusive these thoughts are for us. It may feel like you are the only one with disturbing and unwanted

thoughts that seem to pop up at the worst times. Know that you are not, and that this experience is common. You don't have to buy into ITs and suffer through the mental pain.
We cannot stress this enough: managing your reaction and response to these thoughts is the key to effectively managing your emotional discomfort.

THERE'S NOTHING WRONG WITH YOU

Having intrusive thoughts does not mean that you are or will be a bad person, or that you are going "crazy." Just by reading this book, we know you are committed to living your fullest life. You are ready to face the discomfort of intrusive thoughts in service of what you care about. People facing this fear usually have many strengths that help them to move forward. The fact that you are attentive to things going wrong implies kindness, care for self and others, and integrity, to name a few. Offer yourself kindness and understanding for your struggle with intrusive thoughts. There is no problem with you. The only problem here is that you are taking your intrusive thoughts too seriously instead of recognizing them for the brain spam that they are.

THEY'RE NOT SUBCONSCIOUS DESIRES

Our brains are wired to pump all kinds of information to the forefront of our minds. Your brain wants to keep you as safe as possible, so it informs you of all the terrible things that may go wrong. The brain produces detailed thoughts or images so that it can also inform us of all the ways to solve potential problems. This is especially true for things or people who are important to us. Our brains want to protect what we value the most. The important thing to remember is that intrusive thoughts do not represent deep, unresolved issues or desires. In fact, they are a natural process of your brain, preparing you to safely and successfully move toward the things that mean the most to you.

CHECK-IN

Take a moment to pause. You may notice feelings of frustration, confusion, anxiety, embarrassment, guilt, or shame. You made it this far, and we are right here with you.

Think of a situation in your life where your intrusive thoughts seem to pop up without fail. Gently invite this situation and these thoughts to your mind. Can you actually feel the emotional discomfort in your body? Good. We want you to feel whatever you feel in this moment.

Now, say to yourself out loud: *This feels painful right now.*

Now, say to yourself out loud: *Pain is universal. Other people feel pain, too.*

Now, say to yourself out loud: *I can be patient and kind to myself when I need it the most.*

Stay in this state of self-compassion for a moment longer. You deserve it. Feel free to come back to this exercise after each chapter or whenever you need it most.

Breaking the Cycle

Over the next few chapters, you will read about different techniques that will assist you in developing a new relationship with your thoughts—one that is based on relating to them as harmless brain hiccups versus critical messaging. We are confident that with all this new learning, brain rewiring, and new tools in your toolbox, you will have everything you need to break the cycle of intrusive thoughts.

CHAPTER THREE

Causes of Intrusive Thoughts

ALTHOUGH THE EXPERIENCE OF INTRUSIVE thoughts is extremely common, when they co-occur with other symptoms, such as ongoing sadness, decreased life satisfaction, and impaired functioning, you are more likely to be experiencing a mental health condition. The most common mental health conditions associated with intrusive thoughts are anxiety disorders such as Generalized Anxiety Disorder (GAD), Social Anxiety Disorder (SAD), Panic Disorder, and Obsessive-Compulsive Disorder (OCD).

Triggering Experiences and Circumstances

The content of intrusive thoughts varies depending on our life circumstances, values, and recent life events. For example, if you are doing a quick scan of the day's news and note a disturbing article about a mother who drove off a bridge with her children in the car, you may have an intrusive thought later about losing control and driving your family off a bridge. Or if you have experienced a traumatic event in your life, such as surviving a school shooting, and then you hear of a recent school shooting, you may be more likely to have intrusive thoughts related to the trauma surface shortly after contact with this triggering information.

Before proceeding with this chapter, we want to caution any reader that has a tendency toward health anxiety that your anxious mind may get triggered when reading about mental health conditions. If you find your brain getting flooded with thoughts such as, *Oh no, that sounds like me*, or, *I have even more problems than I knew I had* as you read this chapter, it is time to take a time-out and ground yourself in the present moment. Try to read with an active, curious stance versus a panicked perspective.

GENERALIZED ANXIETY DISORDER

If you are experiencing generalized anxiety disorder (GAD), you may be susceptible to frequent, out-of-control worrying. Worries can be defined as thoughts and images that involve the perception of risk and which are experienced as somewhat uncontrollable (Borkovec et al., 1998). Worries relate more to everyday life, such as fear of getting sick or fear of financial ruin, rather than other more extreme intrusive thought content, but worries are no less disruptive. In fact, the experience of frequent worrying can more negatively impact your ability to accomplish key life tasks because you may believe that you need to spend precious moments listening to, or being bossed around by, the worry because it points out all of the things that can and will most likely go wrong.

The hardest part of pushing past frequent worrying is that this kind of thinking has a way of parading around as effective problem solving. Those experiencing GAD often believe they are accomplishing something by sitting around worrying. They can feel like this negative thinking has protective powers, and if they give it up they are tempting fate and making the feared negative outcome more likely. If you experience GAD symptoms, you may hold the inaccurate belief that engaging in worrying will protect you, because if you review all the potential worst-case scenarios, you will be more likely to effectively manage and survive these negative events, should they occur. But there is no preparing for sickness, financial ruin, loss of a loved one, or any other painful life event. When hard events occur, we all just have to move through the unique pain of the situation. Planning out how you will handle endless catastrophes only increases your suffering and does nothing to increase your coping resources. We will share with you tips and tools to enhance your coping resources in later chapters of this book.

Common Intrusive Thoughts and Images:

- Thoughts/images of losing your job, getting fired, financial ruin, becoming homeless, destroying your family's financial opportunities, etc.
- Thoughts/images of you or your loved ones getting sick

Common Compulsions and Safety Behaviors:

- Worrying/mentally reviewing how each negative outcome could unfold and how you would try to cope with these catastrophic events

- Checking to make sure everything is okay (with your friends, partner, bank account, boss, etc.)
- Avoidance of the sources of worry (email, bank account, work project, etc.) so that you don't have to interact with the area of life that brings on anxiety

SOCIAL ANXIETY DISORDER

If you are experiencing social anxiety disorder (SAD), you may experience difficulty moving on from past mistakes. You may experience frequent intrusive thoughts and worries around losing control and doing something embarrassing. The key clinical criterion for social anxiety disorder is extreme fear of judgment. For those experiencing SAD, the fear of being perceived as flawed or lacking leads to avoidance of activities and life events, excessive time reviewing social performance to determine a "social blunder," and decreased life satisfaction. Their world gets smaller and smaller as they prioritize minimizing contact with social judgment over living life to the fullest.

Common Intrusive Thoughts and Images:
- Thoughts/images of saying or doing something embarrassing
- Thoughts/images of writing something embarrassing

Common Compulsions and Safety Behaviors:
- Mentally reviewing to make sure you did not make a mistake or say something embarrassing
- Checking or obtaining reassurance from an external party to make sure you did not make a social blunder
- Overly planning or rehearsing for how you will handle an upcoming social interaction
- Avoidance of social situations

PANIC DISORDER

The key clinical criterion for panic disorder is fear of the experience of panic attacks. A panic attack is simply your brain experiencing a false alarm and determining you are in danger when you are actually safe and sound.

Most people will experience a panic attack at some point in their life. A smaller percentage of the population will have a phobic reaction to panic attacks and any accompanying symptoms of fear and anxiety. Most people experience intrusive thoughts on occasion but only a small number take them seriously and work themselves into a pretzel by engaging in any and all behaviors to avoid contact with these thoughts. The same is true when it comes to panic attacks and panic disorder. In fact, panic disorder can be thought of as fear of fear, anxiety about anxiety, or panic about panic. A key predictor of panic disorder is anxiety sensitivity. Anxiety sensitivity means you are more impacted by the sensations of anxiety and are more likely to engage in behaviors to avoid bringing on these uncomfortable feelings. You are also more likely to interpret the experience of anxiety as something dangerous and unbearable, rather than simply uncomfortable but tolerable.

Common Intrusive Thoughts and Images:
- Thoughts/images of dying
- Thoughts/images of going "crazy"
- Thoughts/images of "losing control"

Common Compulsions and Safety Behaviors:
- Body scanning to determine if you are ill or dying
- Overly accessing health care due to physical sensations associated with anxiety and panic (chest tightness, rapid heartbeat, shortness of breath, dizziness, nausea, etc.)

- Mental checks to determine if you still have proper brain functions
- Avoidance of situations or places where panic attacks have occurred in the past
- Avoidance of activities that may cause the same physiological responses of panic attacks, such as exercising or going on a car ride

OBSESSIVE-COMPULSIVE DISORDER

The frequent experience of intrusive thoughts is a key diagnostic characteristic of obsessive-compulsive disorder (OCD). By definition, OCD is an anxiety disorder characterized by persistent intrusive thoughts that evoke anxiety and emotional discomfort. In order to diminish anxiety related to bothersome thoughts or obsessions, a person struggling with OCD will perform overt or covert neutralizing acts in the form of compulsions. Compulsions can either be external (such as handwashing) or internal (such as mentally reviewing a past moment to determine if you did something wrong).

Common Intrusive Thoughts or Images:
- Thoughts/images of dying
- Thoughts/images of causing harm to others (stabbing your spouse, infecting a friend with a virus, sexually assaulting a child, running over pedestrians with a car, etc.)
- Thoughts/images of losing control and harming yourself
- Thoughts/images of accidentally causing harm to others by being irresponsible and forgetting to complete a task, such as forgetting to lock the door and someone breaks in and murders your family, or forgetting to turn off the stove and your home burns down

- Thoughts/images of engaging in sexually inappropriate acts
- Thoughts/images of engaging in blasphemous acts

Common Compulsions and Safety Behaviors:

EXTERNAL COMPULSIONS	INTERNAL/MENTAL COMPULSIONS
Washing	Mentally reviewing
Checking	Mentally neutralizing a "bad thought" with a good thought
Counting	
Tapping	Scanning body to assess for inappropriate sensations
Seeking external reassurance	
	Counting
Confessing	
Googling/researching	Thinking things in a "just right" way

POST-TRAUMATIC STRESS DISORDER AND TRAUMA

If you are experiencing post-traumatic stress disorder (PTSD) or trauma, you may have endured or witnessed a traumatic event that involved actual or threatened death (to yourself or others). A traumatic event is one that causes physical and/or psychological distress, usually resulting in intense fear and anxiety. People with PTSD often experience repeated unwanted thoughts, memories, and feelings of fear, anger, guilt, and shame. You may also tend to avoid certain people or places and see changes in your mood and thinking. Trauma-related intrusive thoughts usually correlate to the particular event during which this trauma occurred. Thoughts, feelings, images, sounds, and smells can call upon a person's worst memories about the incident. People with PTSD are stuck in their upsetting memories. These experiences are intrusive and unwanted, and interfere with present-moment functioning.

Common Intrusive Thoughts or Images:
- Thoughts/images of past physical abuse
- Thoughts/images about encountering a perpetrator
- Thoughts/images of an abuser's face and bodily scent
- Sounds of bombs going off nearby

Common Compulsions and Safety Behaviors:
- Immediately picturing faces of loved ones
- Calling family members to check on their safety
- Checking for safety in all situations
- Avoidance of loud noises

Intrusive Thoughts by the Numbers

- Approximately 1.2 percent of the population meet clinical criteria for obsessive-compulsive disorder (OCD)
- Approximately 3.1 percent of the population meet clinical criteria for generalized anxiety disorder (GAD)
- Approximately 2.7 percent of the population meet clinical criteria for panic disorder
- Approximately 6.8 percent of the population meet clinical criteria for social anxiety disorder (SAD)
- Approximately 1.3 to 10 percent of the population meet clinical criteria for illness anxiety disorder
- Approximately 3.5 percent of the population meet clinical criteria for post-traumatic stress disorder (PTSD)
- Approximately 2.8 percent of the population meet clinical criteria for bipolar disorder
- Approximately 4.4 percent of the population meet clinical criteria for attention-deficit hyperactivity disorder (ADHD)
- Approximately 8.4 percent of the population meet clinical criteria for substance abuse disorder

BIPOLAR DISORDER

If you are experiencing bipolar disorder, you may have unusual shifts in mood, energy, and concentration on daily tasks. You may experience a range of mood and energy, from manic "up" episodes of feeling elated, irritable, and energetic to depressive "down" episodes of feeling sad, indifferent, hopeless, and with low energy. During manic or hypomanic episodes, people may experience racing thoughts, sleep and eat less, rapidly talk about different things, have poor judgment, or engage in risky behaviors. During depressive episodes, people may be more likely to sleep and eat more, feel slowed down or empty, have trouble making decisions, or have little interest in new or previously experienced activities.

Common Intrusive Thoughts or Images:
- Thoughts/images of self-harm or suicide
- Thoughts of self-hatred and self-blame
- Thoughts/images of previous traumas
- Thoughts/images of previous conflicts or negative experiences with others

Common Compulsions and Safety Behaviors:
- Avoidance of triggering images
- Checking history of sent text messages or work emails
- Seeking reassurance from others about status of friendship

ATTENTION-DEFICIT HYPERACTIVITY/ IMPULSIVITY DISORDER

If you are experiencing attention-deficit hyperactivity/ impulsivity disorder (ADHD), you may have trouble paying attention, controlling your impulsivity, or feel overactive, often an experience you've had since you were a child. You might have been called a "daydreamer" or "class clown." You may fidget with your hands or feet or squirm in your seat. You may have others tell you that you talk too much. You may also struggle with core executive functioning skills, such as time management, planning, organization, and starting tasks. You may always be running late to events or finding yourself losing or forgetting important things. A person's impulsivity or inattention may often incur more focused rumination or attention on negative self-talk and intrusive thoughts. Worrisome thoughts and negative thinking account for many of these intrusive thoughts (Abramovitch et al., 2009). It is important to note that ADHD is considered a neurodevelopmental disorder that often lasts into adulthood but originates in childhood.

Common Intrusive Thoughts or Images:
- Thoughts/images of making mistakes or forgetting things
- Thoughts/images of impulsively lying to others
- Thoughts/images of previous failures

Common Compulsions and Safety Behaviors:
- Writing down everything in an overly thorough manner
- Mentally reviewing past social interactions
- Ruminating over past mistakes to ensure they won't happen again

DEPRESSION AND POSTPARTUM DIFFICULTIES

If you are experiencing depression, you may think negatively about yourself, relationships with others, and your future experiences. You may experience a change in appetite and sleep, low energy and fatigue, difficulty concentrating, and less pleasure doing the things you used to enjoy. You may waver between feelings of intense sadness and emotional numbness. While feeling sad and occasional changes in functioning is typical, experiencing these symptoms for at least two weeks with impaired functioning is considered significant.

Postpartum depression may occur in new mothers experiencing sadness and symptoms after giving birth to children. While you may feel sad or empty during the first few days of motherhood, postpartum depression is a very real issue that evolves into ongoing negative self-talk, pessimistic perspectives, and feelings of hopelessness or worthlessness. This is a common experience for mothers, with one in nine mothers experiencing postpartum depression (Ko et al., 2017).

Common Intrusive Thoughts or Images:
- Thoughts/images of evaluating self in an extreme way, such as being "a worthless human"
- Thoughts/images of past failures and missed opportunities
- Thoughts/images of assuming responsibility and predicting negative outcomes
- Thoughts/images of not loving their baby or causing harm to newborn infant

Common Compulsions and Safety Behaviors:
- Searching for evidence that the problem cannot be resolved
- Checking for flaws in self and perfection in others
- Seeking reassurance from others that you are a good parent

EATING DISORDERS, BODY DYSMORPHIC DISORDER, SUBSTANCE ABUSE, AND MORE

Intrusive thoughts also accompany other mental health disorders. For eating disorders, intrusive thoughts are linked to food and body image. A person becomes preoccupied or stuck on thoughts about eating the right amount or types of food or being the ideal body weight or size.

For those with body dysmorphic disorder, intrusive thoughts center around perceived flaws and specific body parts. Individuals may also have intrusive thoughts about others making fun of their appearance, attractiveness as guaranteed happiness, and about physical imperfections or asymmetrical body features.

Intrusive thoughts preceding substance abuse behaviors may be stuck on past experiences where one feels shame or guilt. There may also be repetitive, intrusive thoughts about stopping the substance abuse behaviors. Many engage in substance use as a maladaptive coping strategy and tend to self-medicate to ease their discomfort and anxiety.

Common Intrusive Thoughts or Images:

- Thoughts/images of yourself with an unwanted body size and others with ideal body size
- Thoughts/images of past experiences linked to feelings of shame and guilt
- Thoughts/images of using substances one last time (knowing that there will be other times)
- Thoughts/images of particular body parts as majorly flawed, accompanied by feelings of disgust

Common Compulsions and Safety Behaviors:

- Eating more/less, or engaging in purging behaviors
- Intensely engaging in exercise until achieving a "just right" feeling
- Seeking reassurance from others that a certain amount of substance use is "normal"
- Avoiding situations that evoke shame or guilt
- Repetitively checking particular body parts in the mirror
- Continuously comparing self with others' body size or body parts

CHECK-IN

Pause for a moment. Notice any intrusive thoughts that may be surfacing as we discuss different mental health conditions. You may have noticed feelings of worry, panic, sadness, confusion, or discomfort. Gently approach this with curiosity.

Which intrusive thoughts showed up for you? Here are some common ITs:

- Oh no, that sounds like me.
- This proves I really am crazy.
- There are so many things wrong with me.
- This is hopeless. I am so flawed.

Which compulsions or safety behaviors showed up for you? Here are some common ones:

- Reviewing symptoms of these disorders and continuously checking to see how similar your experience is. (Note: one time for psychoeducation and learning is appropriate; however, more than one assessment and it likely has become an unhelpful behavior.)
- Asking others if they notice these things about you
- Searching online for more information on these disorders or finding specific answers to specific questions about them
- Searching online or asking others in hopes of finding a similar story with a predictable (hopefully successful) outcome

Did you notice any of these intrusive thoughts or compulsions? Do you experience others you could add to the list? Keep an eye out for them as you bravely continue your journey through this book.

No Matter the Thought, and No Matter the Disorder, You Can Break Free

No matter the thought or disorder, you can become "unstuck" and live a fulfilling and meaningful life. In the next chapter, we will provide you with strategies and techniques that can help you to break free from these thoughts.

CHAPTER FOUR

How to Break Free

THIS CHAPTER WILL GIVE YOU AN OVERVIEW of the most effective therapeutic modalities for breaking free from intrusive thoughts. You may have heard of some of these techniques and may have even tried them in the past, or they may be completely new. Either way, we encourage you to keep an open mind as we explore the different therapies.

Cognitive Behavioral Therapy for Intrusive Thoughts

All the evidence-based strategies for managing intrusive thoughts introduced in this chapter fall within the *cognitive behavioral therapy* (CBT) framework, a gold standard in psychological treatment. CBT is considered the primary therapeutic treatment for youth and adults with mild to moderate symptoms of anxiety and OCD, although for more severe symptoms of OCD, research suggests that a combination of CBT and medication is most effective (Geller et al., 2012; Koran et al., 2007).

CBT
Short-Term, Action-Oriented Evidence-Based Treatments

Acceptance Commitment Therapy (ACT)	Mindfulness Training	Exposure Response Prevention (ERP)

THE BASICS OF COGNITIVE BEHAVIORAL THERAPY (CBT)

CBT is a short-term, action-oriented, evidence-based approach, based in the idea that thoughts, feelings, and behaviors are interconnected. Your thoughts affect how you feel and what you do (or avoid doing), your feelings affect what you think and do, and your behaviors affect what you think and how you feel. In short, what you tell yourself or believe about a situation affects how you feel, plus the next action you decide to take. Problems arise when unhelpful ways of thinking and ineffective behavioral patterns take over and become automatic. CBT helps you examine your thinking, feeling, and behavior patterns so you can change or challenge them to be more realistic, balanced, and helpful.

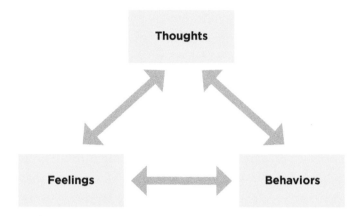

CBT can help you learn to identify faulty thinking patterns or errors that keep you stuck, known as *cognitive distortions*. For example, the thought *I feel dumb, so I must be dumb and everyone thinks I am dumb* has three hidden cognitive distortions: 1) emotional reasoning (*It feels true so it must be true.*); 2) labeling (*I must be dumb.*); and 3) mind reading (*Everyone is thinking it.*). CBT also helps you explore your *core beliefs*, ideas that feel certifiably true to you and affect your perspective on and interpretation of situations you encounter. Common core beliefs include *I am lazy, I am unworthy*, and *Nothing will ever change for me.* You can see how these examples may feel true and keep you feeling stuck. You will learn more about cognitive distortions and core beliefs in chapter 6.

Through CBT you will engage in behavioral experiments, or exposures, to see if what you predict is true. You usually learn that this belief is untrue and unhelpful, and is probably keeping you from important things in your life. However, sometimes your prediction is true. This might sound like your worst nightmare confirmed, but trust us: New learning is happening in your brain, working to get you closer to a life led by *you*, instead of your intrusive thoughts and emotions. You will learn that although it felt uncomfortable to receive a critical comment at work, you can absolutely handle the discomfort and still be a wonderful, successful employee. Instead of taking your thoughts and feelings at face value, you can change your relationship to them and better evaluate their validity.

Recall that intrusive thoughts bring on anxiety and discomfort when 1) you believe they are likely to be true or likely to happen, and/or 2) you think that just having the thought means something about your character or intentions. Through CBT, you can learn to identify unhelpful thinking and behavior patterns by challenging and reframing your thoughts and engaging in a behavioral experiment, or exposure, to weaken that link between intrusive thoughts and anxiety.

EXPOSURE AND RESPONSE PREVENTION THERAPY (ERP)

Exposure and response prevention therapy (ERP) is an essential component of CBT for intrusive thoughts, and especially for OCD. In addition to what you have learned, ERP asks you to gradually confront your feared intrusive thoughts at a pace that feels like a challenge to you—not too easy, not too hard. The goal is to *intentionally* evoke anxiety and discomfort through experience. Through inhibitory learning, your brain will learn that 1) you can tolerate discomfort (inherently easing your anxiety), 2) anxiety won't last forever, and 3) you can make it through even your worst fears without having to shield yourself with compulsions. Research about ERP has demonstrated it is highly effective for managing intrusive thoughts in children and adults (Law et al., 2019).

The first step of ERP is to list all your intrusive thoughts and identify your compulsions and safety behaviors. Then, rank your feared thoughts and avoided situations, forming your *exposure hierarchy*. Next, choose an exposure task that has you confront your feared intrusive thoughts. Finally, while engaged in the exposure task, your goal is not to do anything that may ease your discomfort. No compulsions or safety behaviors allowed! If you cannot stop compulsions altogether, an alternative gradual approach to discontinuing them gives you options to 1) delay, 2) slow down, 3) shorten, or 4) change the way you engage in the behavior.

Exposure tasks require creativity; you can even have fun with them. Although you can engage in exposure tasks on your own, we recommend having an ERP therapist by your side who can assist you in creatively tailoring exposures, provide accountability and encouragement, and set you up for success. You may feel alarmed at what ERP asks you to do. You aren't alone! It may feel odd that you are asked to do things that bother you, but aren't you already feeling bothered by and uncomfortable because of your intrusive thoughts? What you resist persists, and this is definitely the case for intrusive thoughts. ERP flips the power around so that *you* decide how and when you'll cue up those thoughts and start changing your relationship with them.

ACCEPTANCE AND COMMITMENT THERAPY (ACT)

Acceptance and commitment therapy (ACT) is an approach that emphasizes accepting your intrusive thoughts and feelings rather than putting all of your energy into trying to change them. Accepting thoughts does not mean that you believe them, give in to them, or let them take over. It means you are open to and accept the fact that these thoughts are present, without trying to do anything to change this reality. ACT also puts forth the idea that emotional pain is universal, and we as humans are guaranteed to experience it. However, we add a layer of suffering onto the pain when we try to change what is or stay stuck in wishing that things would be different than they are in the present moment. Commitment to your values, or what is most important to you, serves as a guiding light out of the suffering and into a fulfilling life.

ACT promotes psychological flexibility, which offers you stability, perspective, and adaptability in moments of suffering. This involves separating from and creating space between you and your thoughts and feelings, making your ITs less believable and less likely that you will derive personal meaning from them. Staying in the moment helps you experience the here and now, and not feel so stuck in unhelpful thoughts about the past or future. Identifying your values and then intentionally engaging in them is what contributes to a fulfilling life not dominated by your intrusive thoughts. ACT has gained more popularity over the past two decades and is a well-supported treatment in managing intrusive thoughts for adolescents and adults (Bluett et al., 2014; Halliburton et al., 2015).

MINDFULNESS TRAINING

Mindfulness training plays a key role in tackling intrusive thoughts and increasing your awareness. This aspect of therapy focuses on a nonjudgmental approach to thoughts and feelings; they are not "good" or "bad," they just are. The goal is to acknowledge their presence and to let them continue to ebb and flow naturally without getting stuck on them. Mindfulness asks you to stay in the present moment to better access your full range of experience without trying to react to or change it. This practice can help to make intrusive thoughts feel less intrusive and jarring.

With mindfulness, you are open to seeing what thoughts and feelings show up, and then you won't be as surprised or shocked when unwanted or strange thoughts appear. If you do not judge your thoughts and feelings as "good" or "bad," then you do not extract meaning from them, helping to break that chain between intrusive thoughts and anxiety. Research highly supports the use of this therapeutic technique for managing intrusive thoughts, plus a variety of other mental health conditions (Hanstede et al., 2008; Hofmann et al., 2010).

Working your mindfulness muscle can be challenging. Like any skill, mindfulness meditation requires commitment and practice. You are not turning off your thoughts; you are tuned in to and aware of your thinking. Your only job is to notice your thoughts, feelings, physical sensations, and the world around you. Notice when and where your mind wanders. This is supposed to happen. Then gently bring your awareness back to something you can feel or see right now.

You may be thinking, *What if this opens the floodgates to every single one of my intrusive thoughts?* You may notice some or all pop up in your mind, but that means you are doing exactly what you need to. Acknowledge and label it as an intrusive thought and stay curious about which thought (intrusive or not) shows up next.

For the next 30 seconds, challenge yourself to close your eyes and be curious about what thoughts come. See if you can welcome them and say "hi," label them as just a thought, not good or bad, and say "goodbye" as the next thought comes to your mind.

Sometimes Medication Helps

You may be wondering if medication could help treat your intrusive thoughts. The answer to this is personal, depending on your symptoms, diagnosis, and how your intrusive thoughts impact your functioning. If you struggle to complete daily life tasks, you may want to meet with a psychiatrist or talk with your primary care provider to discuss your options. Antidepressant medications known as selective serotonin reuptake inhibitors (SSRIs) are commonly used to treat intrusive thoughts. Common SSRIs include duloxetine (Cymbalta), paroxetine (Paxil), sertraline (Zoloft), fluvoxamine (Luvox), fluoxetine (Prozac), and escitalopram (Lexapro).

Activate Your Motivation Muscle

CBT and exposure call on you to approach instead of avoid uncomfortable situations. It won't be easy and probably won't be the part of your day you look forward to most. In these moments, you can activate and strengthen your Motivation muscle to help you jump-start a task, instead of avoiding and dreading it. Your mental muscles need exercise just like any muscle in your body. The more you activate your Motivation muscle to help you approach exposure tasks, the easier it will be to complete them. Focus on your next small step, count backward from 5, and go! Each time you do this (even for monotonous tasks, like brushing your teeth) it will become more natural. The hardest part of any task is starting, and your Motivation muscle and helpful coaching will assist you.

CHECK-IN

Notice any resistance or hesitation as you venture out of your comfort zone into a new strategy. Thoughts may come up such as *I can't do it, Why do I suck at this?* or *This won't help*. Resistance may show up as emotions such as nervousness, fear, or irritability, or in your body as a headache, stomachache, or putting down this book and doing something else. It is okay that your mind and body are doing this right now. You are committing to something unfamiliar, uncertain, and probably scary.

Pause and take a moment to ask yourself:

- *Why did I start trying this new strategy?*
- *Why am I reading this book?*
- *What matters to me most, and how have ITs gotten in the way of this before?*

Now, refocus and plan your next steps: read the next word, then the next sentence, and notice the pages between your fingers as you continue, even through the resistance from your mind and body. Not everything works for everyone, so watch out for tendencies to mentally beat yourself up. Know that it is common for resistance to show up when starting something new. Come back to this exercise when you feel that you can.

What Does Recovery Look Like?

Managing intrusive thoughts means learning not only to tolerate, but also to be playful with uncomfortable ideas and images in your mind, instead of reacting to them. You will know that you have broken free from intrusive thoughts when you pay more attention to the important things around you, and less on trying to dispel or decrease your discomfort. You will even learn to grow bored of your intrusive thoughts, and to take a curious approach to them, asking, *I wonder which scary image will come* up next, or, *Let's see how long this "delightful" thought decides to stick around.* You will no longer allow these thoughts to be in charge, derailing your plans as they have before.

Keep in mind that there will be bumps and times when your thoughts feel stickier than before. Don't be alarmed. This is the natural progression of improvement. You will have the tools to continue and manage your thoughts and feelings. You may also wonder: *If I tackle one intrusive thought, will I have to start over on the next one?* We are so glad you asked. The truth is that behind all the work you have done to break free from those initial intrusive thoughts are overarching principles that will carry over into your journey with the next ones. You can never be at "square one" again.

WILL I ALWAYS HAVE THESE THOUGHTS?

The short answer is yes. You, along with just about all humans, will experience occasional intrusive thoughts. The good news is that your experience will change. You may even notice the tone and content of your intrusive thoughts change, and eventually they won't produce that once-familiar intense stab of discomfort. Remember that the intrusive thought itself is not the problem; it is your reaction to it and how stuck you become in your experience of discomfort.

HOW LONG DOES IT TAKE TO BREAK FREE?

Thank your mind for this question, as it so desperately wants to feel better. Know that breaking free from intrusive thoughts is an individual journey, but one that you will succeed at. Rewiring learned pathways in your brain takes time and, with practice, you will be forming new pathways that assist you in more easily engaging in different actions, and not reacting to ITs. A typical course of CBT for intrusive thoughts can last 12 to 16 weeks, although some choose to continue therapy for additional support and to maintain treatment gains. Most people start seeing improvements after the first few weeks.

WHAT DO COPING SKILLS LOOK LIKE?

We want to stress that effective coping skills for intrusive thoughts are not purely distractions from your discomfort. Instead of thinking, *Oh no! There's that intrusive thought again. Quick, do something else so I don't have to feel gross,* we'll have you thinking, *Well, well, well . . . there's that intrusive thought again. Thanks for injecting that lovely, gruesome image of me falling off the balcony and splattering on the sidewalk. I'm going to give you a moment of my time, acknowledge your presence, and then I'm going to refocus on the things that are important to me right now, like finishing my breakfast.*

Although that may feel overly simplistic right now, we promise that you will get into the habit of acknowledging these thoughts without having to do anything about them, then getting back to your life. You will acclimate to this new exposure-based lifestyle and it will get easier the more you practice opening up to and intentionally welcoming your intrusive thoughts.

Strategies and Techniques

In part 2, the strategies for breaking free from intrusive thoughts require your commitment and practice. Because you have read to this point, we know you are determined to make a change. The practice requires use of your Motivation muscle (see the Check-In on page 49). Set aside time to intentionally approach these new strategies. Think of this as an investment in your mental health and a fulfilling life. Just like going to the gym to improve or maintain your physical health, you are investing your time and energy into exercising for your mental health. Our advice to you is to *keep at it, even if it feels uncomfortable.* We aren't asking you to be perfect—far from it. In fact, we need you to experience discomfort to properly have your brain learn and rewire its reactions. When you feel discomfort while practicing these strategies, you are well on your way to rewiring your brain to break free from intrusive thoughts.

PART TWO

STRATEGIES AND TECHNIQUES FOR BREAKING FREE

If you are reading this, you are now armed with a solid understanding of what intrusive thoughts are and, more importantly, what they are not. You may be thinking that it is not a big deal that you have stuck with us, but that would not be giving yourself enough credit. The work of reading this book required making contact with a lot of triggering, scary words that likely brought on feelings of anxiety. That very same ability to tolerate emotional discomfort while proceeding is the key to freedom from your intrusive thoughts.

CHAPTER FIVE

Mindfully Attend to Your Intrusive Thoughts

ENHANCED MINDFULNESS ALLOWS FOR MORE time making contact with the present moments and less engaging in the noise and distraction generated by your easily distractible mind. Mindfulness-based exercises involve noting your thoughts, feelings, and sensations, then gently bringing your attention back to the current moment. It is important to note that mindfulness training is not synonymous with relaxation exercises or a massage. It is hard work that will feel more like a gym workout. But just as you always feel better after you exercise your body, you will always feel better after you work out your mind through mindfulness training.

Mindfulness Training for Intrusive Thoughts

Working out your mindfulness mental muscle simply involves continually returning your attention back to the present moment and not letting your mind get swept up in mental noise. Imagine that your overactive mind is a stimuli-seeking puppy, always ready to explore the world around it. Mindfulness is like a harness and leash for your "puppy mind." Instead of being dragged in all different directions, you can choose the direction to move your mind, and gently guide it along your values-driven path. Mindfulness training will give you more of an understanding of how to calmly and compassionately guide your "puppy mind" past the numerous distractions that surface each second, so you can proceed and attend to activities that are the most important to *you*!

Mindfulness training will assist you in fostering a willingness to experience all thoughts, memories, and sensations as they are, without attempting to avoid, alter, or escape them. This form of acceptance counters the need to struggle with uncomfortable feelings, thoughts, and life circumstances. In Georg H. Eifert and John P. Forsyth's book *Acceptance and Commitment Therapy for Anxiety Disorders*, they write: "Freedom comes from being liberated from the losing battle against oneself and one's life experience. You cannot fight against yourself and win." By engaging in the mindfulness exercises introduced in this chapter, you will come to see all mental material, such as thoughts, feelings, and sensations, as passing natural events rather than dangerous warning signs of your "deviant, disturbed" nature.

MINDFULNESS TRAINING AS A CLINICAL INTERVENTION FOR ITs

As discussed, those struggling with intrusive thoughts tend to mistake an uncomfortable thought for a dangerous one, then apply thought suppression to avoid the feared consequences of having this thought. Unfortunately, this only leads to increased thought frequency, and this cycle is only strengthened with repetition.

To break this cycle, you must teach your brain that there is nothing dangerous or catastrophic about having an intrusive thought. By disengaging from thought avoidance and control strategies, and allowing yourself to directly experience an intrusive thought, you will teach your brain that thoughts, impulses, and images are not so important that they must be corrected or neutralized. Instead, they can safely be ignored and dismissed. Repeatedly experiencing instead of avoiding uncomfortable thoughts will help you come to see your intrusive thoughts as random brain noise rather than meaningful information. Mindfulness training exercises will assist you in learning to accept your thoughts, enhancing your ability to disengage from them and engage in your life.

HOW FELLOW TRAVELERS USED MINDFULNESS TRAINING IN THE STRUGGLE WITH THEIR INTRUSIVE THOUGHTS

Our client "Tanisha" (page 11) struggled with intrusive thoughts and images of inappropriately touching her students. She would return home from work every day and spend several hours sitting on the couch, staring into space, reviewing all of the moments of her day to assess, check, and then recheck to see if she crossed any lines or did anything inappropriate. Tanisha experienced extreme emotional distress in reaction to her intrusive thoughts. She was emotionally exhausted and felt depleted of all her energy. In session, Tanisha described how she recently found herself having little time or energy left at the end of the day to keep up with her basic life tasks and home management requirements. Together, we decided on the homework assignment of mindfully spending 30 minutes a day tidying up her apartment after she returned home from work.

By selecting a life task that was important to her and practicing and completing this task no matter what thought showed up, Tanisha grabbed the reins of her life from her intrusive thoughts and no longer let her wandering "puppy mind" call the shots. Tanisha was also teaching her brain that just because intrusive thoughts demand her full attention, she does not have to give in to them. She understood that she need not stop all her important life activities to engage in the mental compulsions of analyzing and reviewing. She could still move forward, even if she had to take the intrusive thoughts with her as she engaged in valued living.

HOW CAN MINDFULNESS HELP YOU TO BREAK FREE FROM YOUR INTRUSIVE THOUGHTS?

You relinquish your power to your intrusive thoughts by taking them seriously and engaging with them as though they reflect critical information. You also empower them by fighting with them or judging yourself for having them. And as discussed, the more you fight with your intrusive thoughts or have an extreme negative reaction when they surface, the more super-charged they will be. Each time you engage in a mindfulness training exercise, you are strengthening your ability to place your attention on aspects of your life that are most important to you, instead of your intrusive thoughts.

STRATEGIES AND TECHNIQUES

1. Mindful Cleaning

1. Pick an area of your house or apartment and a cleaning task.

2. Set a timer for 30 minutes.

3. Place your attention on this task.

4. Notice when your attention wanders.

5. Gently and nonjudgmentally bring your attention back to your cleaning task.

6. Repeat every time your "puppy mind" once again wanders off.

As mentioned previously, completing this task helped Tanisha to learn how to move forward with carrying out activities that were important to her without allowing her "puppy mind" to give in to the demands of her intrusive thoughts.

2. How Does Your Emotional Reaction Impact Your Anxiety Level?

1. Set a timer for 2 minutes.

2. Intentionally think about an intrusive thought you have struggled with recently.

3. For the next 2 minutes place your attention on anything except the intrusive thought.

4. After the timer goes off, rate how anxious you feel from 0 to 10 (0 being not at all, 10 being very anxious).

5. Next, set the timer for another 2-minute period.

6. Over the 2-minute period, repeatedly bring forth the intrusive thought, without interruption. We recommend that you say the intrusive thought out loud or write it down, over and over again for maximum impact.

7. After the timer goes off, rate how anxious you feel from 0 to 10 (0 being not at all, 10 being very anxious).

Were you able to avoid thinking about your intrusive thought once you primed yourself to think about it? Even though you may be successful initially, the thought will always return stronger every time. The first step in changing your emotional reaction to your intrusive thoughts is to practice mindfully observing them, then letting them pass on their own.

3. Mindfully Observing Your Intrusive Thoughts

Mindfully observing your intrusive thoughts is like watching a parade go by from the viewing stand. But once you find yourself getting on one of the floats, you can catch yourself overly engaging with an intrusive thought and gently remind yourself, *Oops, I just joined the parade. It is time to return to the viewing stand and simply wait for the next thoughts to surface.*

1. Set a timer for 5 minutes.
2. Begin by focusing your attention on your breath, the inhale and the exhale.
3. Whenever an intruding thought, image, or sensation surfaces, notice and label it for what it is.
4. Try to observe each of these intruders with an accepting and curious attitude. Without labeling them as "good" or "bad," just observe them as a bystander looking on.
5. Without pushing them away, allow these thoughts to drift away on their own.
6. After allowing each thought to show itself, simply return your attention back to the breath.
7. Repeat steps 1 through 6 each time you find yourself in a parade of intrusive thoughts.

4. Mindfully Attending to Triggers for Your Intrusive Thoughts

The next step in breaking free from your intrusive thoughts is to understand patterns when they come up. For example, our client "Greg" (page 11), who cared a great deal about his career, found that he would worry about saying something inappropriate to a colleague most often around the time of important business decisions. "Chloe" (page 11) discovered that her intrusive thoughts were tied to shifts in physical health. She was especially vulnerable to them when she hadn't slept, was hungover from drinking, or was close to her period.

Over the next few days, keep a log tracking the time of day when your intrusive thoughts surfaced, including where you were, what you were doing, who you were with, and any other factors, such as how tired or hungry you were. After you've collected a few days' worth of data, note any patterns of when your intrusive thoughts tend to come up. Are they more frequent during certain times of day? Around particular people? When you're doing or thinking particular things?

5. Shifting Attention between Foreground and Background

Listen to the different sounds in your current environment. Perhaps you hear the sound of the air conditioner or the panting sound of your dog breathing by your side. Select one sound and put all of your attention on it. Does it sound louder now that you are fully attending to it? How much was it catching your attention before you started this exercise?

Now pick an attention-demanding exercise to engage in for 1 minute, such as reading something or playing a game on your phone. As you shifted your attention away from the background sound, did the volume seem fainter? As you directly placed your attention on the foreground sound, did it seem louder?

The same concept can be applied to your intrusive thoughts. When you place all of your attention on your intrusive thoughts, they will seem louder. When you place your attention on meaningful living, your intrusive thoughts will quiet down because you are focused on more important aspects of your life.

6. The 3-3-3 Tool for Staying Grounded in Daily Life

The 3-3-3 exercise is a simple but powerful tool to help you quickly calm your mind and return to the present moment. Look around the space you are in, and name three things that you see. Next, name three things that you feel. These are physical sensations, rather than internal emotions. Finally, name three things that you hear. This one might take you a moment. It can be helpful to say the things out loud, but if you're in a public space, you can just say them in your head.

You can repeat this exercise as many times as you need, although our clients often find that doing it even once assists them in returning to the here and now, instead of getting stuck engaging in the mental compulsions of reviewing or analyzing their intrusive thoughts.

7. Attend to Your Body

It's important to become acquainted with your body when it is not consumed by anxiety in reaction to intrusive thoughts. Attending to your body is key to redirecting your energy from ITs and back to the current moment.

At this very moment, tune in to your body. How thirsty do you feel? Are you hungry? Do you notice tension or tightness in any specific spots? What is your posture? Are you sitting with your back straight and your chest open, or is your spine curved and your shoulders hunched forward? When was the last time you stood up or stretched out your limbs?

8. Anchoring Down

We all have a quiet, calm, centered place within ourselves, even when our thoughts are running wild and emotions are high. It's just a matter of learning how to access this center.

Imagine you are in a boat on choppy waters and floating out farther and farther away from land. You need to anchor your boat. This may be a familiar feeling to you, as intrusive thoughts can make us feel out of control and drifting away, from the moment or ourselves. Fear not: Mindfulness is your anchor. Imagine gently releasing an anchor in your mind and watch it slowly sink throughout your body and melt into the bottom of that centered place within you. This is the place where your wisdom lies and mind rests. Where does your anchor land? Perhaps it is in your chest, abdomen, hips, or feet.

9. Mindfulness Meditation Practice

A multitude of guided meditations are available across a variety of downloadable apps. If you want to start meditating without a guide, you can do so by following our simple instructions here.

We recommend sitting up straight on a cushion or chair and placing an object in front of you to focus your gaze. Once you're seated, gently rest your gaze on the object you've placed in front of you. You could part your lips slightly, letting air flow smoothly in and out. Try to bring a completely nonjudgmental awareness to the object. Simply notice its shape and its colors, its shadows and angles. Whenever you start to have judgments or get lost in stories about the object or your own past or future, bring your attention back to your object. Remember, you're not trying to block out thoughts. You are simply learning to notice where your mind goes and to not get caught up in distractions. You are observing your own thoughts, without judgment, then learning to come back to the present moment. We recommend sitting for this meditation for at least 10 minutes.

Remember, just by showing up to your cushion or chair and practicing returning to the present moment, no matter how distracted you may feel, you are rewiring your brain and bringing about the tremendous benefits of meditation.

10. Mindful Eating

Next time you eat, try to do so mindfully without distraction. Take each bite slowly and thoroughly, paying close attention to all the aspects of the food you are consuming: the texture, aroma, and flavor profile. Try not to judge the food as good or bad, just simply describe it using all of your senses (crunchy, cold, salty, spicy, tart, etc.). As you thoroughly chew your food, you may even notice the taste changes as the flavors release.

11. Set a Mindfulness Reminder

To remind you to practice mindfulness throughout your day, we recommend setting automatic reminders that remind you to bring mindful attention to your moment. You can set alarms on your phone or strategically place handwritten reminders that you'll see throughout the day (a note on the coffee maker, in your wallet, on your salad container, etc.). When you see these reminders, gently bring your nonjudgmental attention to what is happening in your current moment and just notice your surroundings, checking in with all of your senses.

12. Mindfulness Mantras

A mantra—a word or phrase that is repeated to help concentration—can be a lifeline back to the present moment. This mantra can hold special meaning or be a simple cue to engage your mindfulness muscles. Set one aside and write it down so you can easily remember it. Next time you are drifting in space with your intrusive thoughts, repeat your mantra until you come back down to earth.

Here are a few examples of mantras to try:

- **Be here now.**
- **All bark and no bite.**
- **Inhale, exhale.**
- **I am enough.**
- **Disconnect to reconnect.**
- **Intrusive thoughts are brain spam.**

13. Draw Your Attention to the Present Moment

Time to get your creative juices flowing. For this exercise you will need a piece of paper and drawing tool.

Begin by focusing your attention on an object in the room. Once you've located your object, start drawing it and try to not spend time planning it out or trying to get it "right." All that matters is mindfully paying attention to all aspects of the object: curves, lines, pattern, texture, shape. The purpose is not to draw the best image, but rather to just notice the object's details. Work that mindfulness muscle and resist the urge to judge your drawing as "good" or "bad."

Observe what it feels like to draw. How much pressure are you applying to your drawing utensil? What does it feel like to press it into the paper?

14. A Song and Dance

Perhaps intrusive thoughts have seized your joy from a fun moment. Today you will reclaim it by singing a song, dancing, or both, all while allowing an intrusive thought to coexist.

The first step is to choose a song that you can sing or dance to for its entire length. Next, think of a recent intrusive thought you've experienced, then play the song. Your job is to stay focused on the words of the song as you sing, or the movement of your body as you dance. If your intrusive thought sticks around, invite it to sing and dance along with you. Allow the whole song to play, then see if you can keep going for a few more minutes. Put the song on repeat or keep singing or dancing with the next song that comes up. Have fun with it!

15. Mindfully Tolerate Discomfort

Rather than getting flooded by emotions or overwhelmed by thoughts, we can mindfully move through difficult moments by focusing our awareness on details of the experience.

For this exercise, watch a news clip or read an article that you find upsetting. As you watch or read the story, observe your emotions, thoughts, and any physical sensations. When your mind wanders or starts spiraling down, use a mindful phrase, such as *"Come back"* to cue yourself to return to present moment sensations. Afterward, write down nonjudgmental, factual descriptions of the emotions, thoughts, and physical sensations you felt during this exercise.

CHAPTER SIX

Explore and Engage with Your Thoughts

NOW THAT YOU HAVE PRACTICED CREATING space between you and your thoughts, you are in a better position to explore them. You will learn to evaluate their accuracy and likelihood through a logical lens. You will also learn to calmly question the importance of your thoughts and determine whether they deserve your time and investment. In this chapter, you will discover ways to identify unhelpful thinking patterns and beliefs that get in the way of your values.

Why Engage with a Stuck Thought?

Intrusive thoughts feel so uncomfortable because they feel so real. Your mind tells you they are: 1) accurate, 2) realistic, 3) could happen any second, and 4) a real danger. In moments of anxiety or heightened emotions, it becomes more difficult for rational thinking to occur in your brain. The prefrontal cortex, or the center of logic and rational thinking, communicates less effectively with your amygdala, the center of anxiety. Learning strategies that use logic to call out the irrationality of your thoughts can strengthen these neural connections, so your amygdala doesn't hijack your rational thinking every time an intrusive thought pops up.

You have probably experienced that desperate feeling to decipher your intrusive thoughts, assigning unnecessary meaning and significance to them, and giving them power. You will now learn to take a calm, neutral approach to thoughts by using your rational mind.

KNOW YOUR TENDENCIES AND PATTERNS

Understanding your intrusive thought patterns will help you break free from them, holding an offensive instead of reactive posture when they surface. Becoming aware of key triggers will help you access your rational mind, challenge your intrusive thoughts, and give you a more realistic, accurate perspective of the situation.

It can be helpful to write down your own tendencies and patterns. Here is an example of our fellow traveler Chloe's (page 11) thought tracking log:

DATE/TIME	Monday at 2 p.m.
SITUATION	Important work meeting with my boss
THOUGHT	What if I stand up and curse out my boss?
FEELING	Terrified, nervous, jumpy
BEHAVIOR	Cross my legs to keep from standing up. Purposefully think nice thoughts about my boss
LINKS TO MY VALUES	- Success - Care for others

WHAT'S IMPORTANT TO YOU?

When you engage your unwanted thoughts, you will find that the things you value most lie beneath them. That's understandably why the thoughts cause so much discomfort. Refocusing on your values helps you gain perspective, identifying what is *actually* important to you, as you break free from intrusive thoughts.

STRATEGIES AND TECHNIQUES

1. Seeing Life Through Your Intrusive Thoughts

Hold your hand in front of your face and notice what you see. How much of your visual field is dominated by your hand? How much else of the world around you can you take in? Now extend your arm, hold your hand up, and notice what you see. How is your visual field affected?

Now, write a recent intrusive thought on a sticky note and place this note on your face, over your eyes. How much of your visual field is taken over by your intrusive thought and how much else of the world can you take in? Hold the sticky note with your intrusive thought in your hand, extend your arm, then put your hand up and notice what you see.

Viewing intrusive thoughts from a new perspective will allow you to notice them, while seeing and attending to so many more important aspects of your life.

2. The Who, What, When, Where, and Whys of Your ITs

Create your own thought-tracking log by noticing and observing your thoughts with curiosity. Try to track your thoughts three times a day (e.g., mealtimes or especially tough "stuck" moments). Watch out for sneaky self-judgments and stick with the facts.

See page 69 for Chloe's example. Make sure to note the following:

1. Date/Time (When)
2. Situation (Where/Who)
3. Thoughts, feelings, behaviors (What)
4. Links to values (Why)

Reflect:

> Are there any common themes?

> Are there any links between thoughts, feelings, behaviors?

> Are there any triggering times of day or situations?

> Are there any values that keep showing up for you?

3. Grow Curious about Your IT Mind

Externalizing your ITs lets you see them accurately. Try to see if you can draw your intrusive thought as a stick figure or cartoon character bully. Give it a silly name, like Mr. All Bark No Bite or Ms. Debbie Downer on Steroids, a comical backstory, or even a ridiculous life motto.

Visualize this character to greet and notice your intrusive thoughts for the next week. Notice your initial discomfort when identifying the intrusive thought and see if they shift as you consider the character you assigned it. Do they lose any of their shock value?

4. Playing with Your ITs

List out as many of your ITs as you can. Start with the first word of your thought, then the next. You could write down just one word for each IT for now.

Starting with just one IT at a time, see how many "Time to Play" activities you can do. Once you've got that down, come back to this exercise and see if you can play around with more than one of your ITs at a time for an extra challenge. Bonus points if you can make it funny!

Time to Play:

> Write it down five times, each time in a different font and size.

> Write it down with your right hand. Now your left hand.

- Write it down backward, word by word and letter by letter.

- Say it backward.

- Sing your thoughts to the tune of your favorite song.

- Draw a symbol or image to represent it.

- Draw a picture of yourself with a thought bubble and write in your IT.

- Create a word cloud of related words and thoughts.

- Write a short and sweet love letter to your IT. ("Dear IT, You are so lovely. Thank you for telling me that I am going to die by suicide and that I hate my life. You always know the right thing to say.")

- Make up a song about your intrusive thoughts.

5. What Are Your ITs' Favorite Thinking Mistakes?
Remember that all unhelpful thinking stems from thinking errors called cognitive distortions. Read through the list and note the answer that feels most true for you to learn which common thinking mistakes your ITs get stuck on.

Which thinking mistakes do you tend to make? Write down your top three and match them to your ITs to discover their distorted perspective.

Intolerance of Uncertainty
Thinking that you must have a 100 percent guarantee of safety or absolute certainty
(I need to know for certain; I cannot handle any doubts or ambiguity.)

All-or-Nothing Thinking
Thinking in extremes or absolutes; no middle ground
(I always make mistakes.)

Magical Thinking
Thinking certain actions will bring on specific outcomes
(If I lose weight, my life will be easier.)

Emotional Reasoning
Thinking if something feels true, then it is true
(I feel dumb, so I must be dumb.)

Thought-Action Fusion (Moral or Likelihood)
Thinking that your unwanted thoughts are equivalent to performing a terrible action (moral) or increases the chance that something terrible will happen (likelihood)
(If I think about death, someone will die.)

Intolerance of Anxiety
Thinking that your anxiety or discomfort will persist forever unless you do something to "fix" it or escape
(I have to get rid of this feeling or else I might go crazy and lose control.)

Catastrophizing
Thinking that one situation will lead to more negative outcomes in the future
(If I don't get this job, I won't ever get another job and I will never be successful.)

Overestimation of Responsibility
Thinking that exaggerates your responsibility for preventing harm to yourself or others; failure to prevent or try to prevent harm is the same thing as causing harm
(I must tell them every detail, or it will be my fault if something goes wrong.)

Overestimation of Threat
Thinking that exaggerates the intensity or occurrence of negative outcomes
(Everything is ruined.)

The "Just Right" Error (Perfectionism)
Thinking that things must be "just right" or perfect to be comfortable
(I will feel better if I do this perfectly or to my standards.)

6. What Does Your IT Tell You to Believe?

Inaccurate and unhelpful core beliefs often underlie intrusive thoughts. Your IT tries to protect you by reminding you of these beliefs, but instead does more damage and only makes you struggle and suffer more.

Check off the core beliefs that feel true to you:

- I am lazy and unmotivated; I always take the easy route.
- I am dumb, stupid, or incompetent.
- I am unworthy, undeserving, or unlovable.
- I am weak, inadequate.
- I am a bad person or abnormal.
- I have to be perfect or feel happy to be normal.
- People are untrustworthy.
- The world is unsafe and dangerous.

Pause and reflect on how you feel as you identify the maladaptive core beliefs that resonate with you. You might notice feelings of sadness or shame. Know that these core beliefs are common and often built into the human experience.

Keep your top three core beliefs in mind as you explore your ITs. You will eventually notice that the same maladaptive core beliefs underlie all of your intrusive thoughts, and understand each thought is the same fear in a new costume.

7. Is Your IT Setting off False Alarms?

Remember that your brain always scans for danger and threats. Sometimes it misfires and determines you or your loved ones are in danger when you are actually safe. An intrusive thought is your brain emitting a false alarm, warning you of a potential catastrophe that is thankfully irrelevant to your current situation.

Whenever an intrusive thought surfaces during the next week, follow these four steps to remember that you are experiencing a false alarm when you are safe.

1. *Acknowledge* your IT sounding the alarm.
2. *Assess* that there is no actual danger in this moment.
3. *Label* it a false alarm.
4. *Refocus* your attention back to the moment.

8. Spam vs. Priority Mail

As we've discussed, intrusive thoughts are simply brain spam pretending to be critical, life-altering information. For this exercise, pretend your mind is an email filtering system and you are determining if emails are spam or priority. Take a look at the sample email subject headers and decide how you would filter these messages.

"Complete Our Survey and Win 2 Million Dollars!!!"

"Your Monthly Utility Bill is Due"

"LOSE 10 LBS. IN 10 DAYS"

"Pls help, in jail and need of money ASAP"

"It's Time to Schedule Your Annual Eye Exam"

▸ **"Check Out This Document!"**

▸ **"An Exclusive Offer Just for You"**

Some of these emails are obviously spam, some require more information gathering, and others brought helpful information to your attention. Similarly, by using your logic and rational reasoning, you can learn to filter ITs as spam that are not actually warning signs of imminent danger.

Think of moments in your life when an intrusive thought provided you with safety. How often were these thoughts actually just spam and not priority mail?

9. Who Is the Better Person?

Think of someone you respect and consider to be a good person or role model. What qualities come to mind when you think of them? Is there something they have done for or with you that you appreciate? Are there moments that stand out to you where their character has prevailed? Pause for a moment to jot down everything you admire about this person.

Did your description include the types of thoughts they have or had? Or were their qualities based on their actions, values, and worthwhile characteristics?

The next time your ITs start to poke around and bother you, pause to reflect on this question: Is someone considered a "better person" because they think good thoughts or because they engage in good behaviors?

10. Take Your ITs to Court

Pretend you are with your ITs in a courtroom where you are the judge. Take a neutral stance and examine the evidence surrounding your ITs. Assess likelihoods and challenge your ITs, then make a verdict: are any cognitive distortions guilty of the "crime" of hijacking your emotions and causing intense discomfort? Remember to call on your rational mind, only using logic and facts in your role as judge—no opinions, assumptions, guesses, or emotional reasoning. See the chart for an example of Greg's (page 11) exercise.

1. **Write down the first IT in question.**
2. **Examine the evidence** *for* **the thought.**
3. **Examine the evidence** *against* **the thought.**
4. **Logically assess the true chance that the thought will become or is true.**
5. **Identify the thinking error culprits (see strategy 5 on page 72) and make a verdict of which ones are to blame for your discomfort.**

INTRUSIVE THOUGHT	What if I suddenly grab my wife's hand and stick it down the garbage disposal?
EVIDENCE FOR	Anything could happen. If I'm mad at her I might feel like doing something to let out my anger.
EVIDENCE AGAINST	I have never, nor do I want to, hurt my wife. I've been mad at her before, and I have resolved it appropriately. It is just a thought, and thoughts do not have to be true.
LIKELIHOOD	2 percent chance I would do this. Low likelihood of occurring.
THINKING ERRORS	Thought-Action Fusion.

11. Turn Unhelpful Thoughts into Helpful Thoughts

Now that you've identified the thinking errors, it's time to find some helpful alternative thoughts that work for you. Your task is to: 1) list your ITs under *Unhelpful Thoughts*, and 2) write down an alternative thought under *Helpful Thoughts* that is realistic, balanced, and accurate. See the chart below for an example. Create your own list on a separate sheet of paper or in a note-taking app on your phone. Try to think of at least three alternative, helpful thoughts.

UNHELPFUL THOUGHTS	HELPFUL THOUGHTS
I always screw up. What if I make a mistake during my work presentation and offend someone?	I make mistakes sometimes because I am human. There is a low chance I would make a big enough mistake to offend someone. Even if I did, I would apologize, and that discomfort won't last forever.

12. Stump Your Stubborn ITs

Sometimes, no matter how hard you try, your ITs won't budge and allow you to out-logic them. Don't battle them with logic if they keep fighting back. Stick with this simple approach that your ITs will have difficulty fighting:

- **This may happen *or* it may not happen.**
- **This may be true *or* it may not be true.**
- **This will either happen *or* it won't happen.**

You are using your rational mind to call out the two possible (in fact, certain) outcomes. There is certainty within the uncertainty, and your ITs stop arguing with that.

13. Rational Mind vs. Emotional Mind

Notice when your emotional mind is in charge. The common thought *"It feels true, so it must be true"* adds extra fuel to your ITs. A rational mind can pause and explore with curiosity and calm, even among feelings of discomfort. See if you can label each thought on the list as coming from your rational mind or emotional mind:

- I just know this will happen.
- This has happened before, so it might happen again.
- Will anything ever go right for me?
- I will for sure do something I regret; I always do these kinds of things.
- It feels like this is inevitable.
- We'll have to see what happens.
- It will probably happen to me; just my luck.
- I cannot handle this feeling.
- This won't last forever, even though it feels like it will.

When you learn to recognize which part of your mind thoughts are stemming from, you can more easily take a step back to acknowledge and challenge them.

14. Unhook from Catastrophic Thinking

Another common source of fuel for ITs is catastrophic thinking. Recall that when this occurs, your mind takes you to the worst-case scenarios. This exercise will help you unhook from catastrophic thinking into more present-moment focused conclusions about yourself and your situation. The goal is to acknowledge that the ITs are insignificant and meaningless. Try to do this for three of your most common catastrophic thoughts.

Hook: *I am going to commit a crime unknowingly, go to jail, lose custody of my kids, and my life will be over!*

Unhook: *I have not committed any crime at this moment. That was a weird "brain blip." I will not buy into my anxiety's insignificant misinterpretations of what is likely to happen.*

Reel into the Present Moment: *I am in my office at work with two important tasks to complete. Nothing dangerous is occurring. I have lost nothing, and my life is not over. I am focusing on my feet on the ground, my hands above the key-board, typing the next word . . .*

15. Thought-Action Fusion (TAF) Experiments

When your thoughts and actions are highly fused, you may believe your inability to control bothersome thoughts is evidence that you will also be unable to control related behaviors. Try the following TAF experiments to defuse this unhelpful and inaccurate belief. Observe what happens. Is there a direct connection between what you think, say, or write down, and your actions or outcomes?

> Think as hard as you can, *Millions of dollars are going to fall down from the sky and land on me,* then notice if this thought created the associated outcome.

> While holding a piece of paper, say aloud, *I am going to give myself a paper cut.*

> Stand on the third step of a staircase and repeat three times: *I want to fall on my face.*

> Sit on a cozy couch, get comfortable, then think as hard as you can, *I am doing crunches and then push-ups and running 5 miles.* Then notice if this thought was enough to set the behaviors in motion.

> Write down *I am going to get a flat tire tomorrow,* and see what happens.

> Think to yourself, on purpose, *I hope my friend gets a cold tomorrow.*

CHAPTER SEVEN

Practice Acceptance

IF FIGHTING PAST INTRUSIVE THOUGHTS released you from them, you would already be free. But as you now know from the information in this book, no matter how hard you try to win the "tug of war" with your intrusive thoughts, they will outmatch your power and strength. This chapter will arm you with acceptance-based tools and strategies so you can live a more peaceful, satisfying life.

The Cost of Fighting with Your Intrusive Thoughts

Struggling with your intrusive thoughts is uncomfortable, with all of those stress hormones pulsing through your body, and it is also a waste of your limited energy supply. When you use your energy to quash these thoughts, you will have less left over for important areas of your life. The negative consequence most frequently associated with a long-term struggle against intrusive thoughts is the valued living you can miss out on while you're engaged with them.

While living a life free of uncomfortable intrusive thoughts is ideal, we will all have moments when they interrupt our experience. When they appear, do not allow them to take control. Simply continue to be involved in what is most important to you.

FROM WRESTLING TO ACCEPTING INTRUSIVE THOUGHTS

At first glance, acceptance appears to imply giving up or rolling over in defeat and letting these thoughts win. But according to the Merriam-Webster dictionary, the true definition of *accept* is to "endure without protest or reaction" and "to recognize as true." Acceptance simply means embracing the reality, or truth, of a situation.

Acceptance is an active posture. Just like you need to activate certain muscles to open your hand and other muscles to close your hand, you must work your acceptance muscle to give up a struggle with things you can't change. It takes effort to attempt to change a situation, and to open yourself up and accept its reality. The good news is that *you* get to decide when it makes sense for you to activate your acceptance muscle and when to activate your change muscle.

COMMON MISCONCEPTIONS ABOUT
FIGHTING WITH INTRUSIVE THOUGHTS

▹ If I try hard enough, I can make them go away.

▹ By not fighting with them, I am agreeing with them.

▹ I can't live a decent life until I extinguish these thoughts.

Deciding not to argue with an intrusive thought does not mean you agree with it. Acceptance is simply awareness of, and not necessarily agreement with, thoughts, people, and situations, without attempting to change them.

STRATEGIES AND TECHNIQUES

1. **How Is the Struggle with Your Intrusive Thoughts Impacting Your Life?**

For each of these three questions, give an answer on a scale of 0 to 10 (0 being the lowest, 10 being the highest), either below or on a separate piece of paper.

How much anxiety and overall emotional distress do you feel about having intrusive thoughts?_____

How often do you avoid certain situations in your life in an effort to avoid intrusive thoughts?_____

How much energy do you spend on an average day trying to extinguish or rid yourself of intrusive thoughts?_____

YOUR TOTAL SCORE: ☐

If you scored from 0 to 14, then the experience of intrusive thoughts is only mildly impairing your ability to live your life to the fullest.

If you scored from 15 to 21, then the experience of intrusive thoughts is moderately impairing your ability to live your life to the fullest.

If you scored from 22 to 30, then the experience of intrusive thoughts is severely impairing your ability to live your life to the fullest.

2. **Assessing Your Energy Output with Acceptance**

Think of a time when you accepted a frustrating event in your life, rather than trying to change or fight it. Now think of a time when you invested emotional energy into fighting with a situation where you could not alter the outcome. Did you experience more emotional distress when you fought with or accepted the discomfort?

3. You and Your Bothersome Beach Ball

Imagine you are standing in the middle of the ocean, and floating in front of you is a beach ball. This beach ball contains all your intrusive thoughts and uncomfortable feelings. You try to throw it away from you, but the wind keeps blowing it back. You try to turn your back to it, but it keeps popping up out of the water around you. Finally, you've had enough and decide to push it under the water where it is harder to see. However, you must continually push as the beach ball keeps floating back up to the surface, and eventually your arms grow tired (after all, you're only human). And when the exhaustion hits (as it always does), that bothersome beach ball will pop right out of the water, hitting you with even more discomfort than you had to begin with.

What do you think would happen if you were to just let that bothersome beach ball float in front of you? It could float away. Notice that the beach ball could not float away if you were holding on to it, pushing it underneath the water and out of sight. You would also probably be less tired, because you wouldn't have to work hard to use that mental and physical energy to keep the ball away. Instead, you would stand there and see that beach ball full of intrusive thoughts and anxious feelings in front of you. Uncomfortable? Yes. Devoting all your mental space and energy to your anxiety and away from what you love? Thankfully, no.

Even when it feels impossible to do, we will be right here as you learn to sit with your bothersome beach ball.

4. You Can Handle Discomfort

Think of all of the uncomfortable feelings you frequently experience. In the last month, recall if you've experienced any of the following:

- **Feeling hot or cold**
- **A paper cut**
- **A headache or migraine**
- **A stubbed toe**
- **A cold or flu**
- **A sprain or a broken bone**
- **Food poisoning**
- **Getting a shot**
- **Dental work**
- **Discomfort during or after a hard workout**

Our clients tend to give their intrusive thoughts way too much credit and power. When you learn to recognize and identify the emotional pain that accompanies them as just another category of discomfort you frequently experience and effectively manage on a daily basis, you are enhancing your brain's ability to activate its "acceptance mental muscle."

5. Tolerating vs. Fighting with Discomfort

Think about your predicted distress over how bad a difficult moment or situation would be, and then how bad it actually was when it happened. Now think about the energy you used trying to avoid inevitable situations. What else could you have used this energy to accomplish?

6. Compare and Contrast

1. Try as hard as you can to make an intrusive thought you had go away.

2. Do a quick body scan to check on how you are feeling in reaction to this struggle with your intrusive thoughts. Start at the top of your head. Notice your face, notice any tension in your forehead, then move down to your shoulders and chest. Do you notice any heaviness? Now move down to your stomach, your legs and finally your feet. Where is your body holding tension?

3. On a scale of 0 to 10, how uncomfortable do you currently feel?

4. Bring on another intrusive thought you recently experienced.

5. Try as hard as you can to tolerate and not fight with the intrusive thought.

6. Stand up (if you are sitting) and stretch out your arms, extending them as far up as they go.

7. Do a quick body scan to check in on how you are feeling in reaction to this struggle with your intrusive thoughts. Do you notice any heaviness? Where is your body holding tension?

8. On a scale of 0 to 10, how uncomfortable do you currently feel?

When you are engaging in the acceptance-based exercises outlined in this chapter (and more importantly, when an intrusive thought surfaces unexpectedly in your everyday life), accept the uncomfortable sensations as much as possible rather than resist what is already unfolding.

7. How Does Fighting with Your Intrusive Thoughts Impact Your Performance?

1. For the next few minutes, try to put all your effort and energy into making an intrusive thought you had go away.

Next, try completing a few tasks that require focus and attention, such as building a house of cards, walking with a book on your head, or doing homework.

2. Think about another intrusive thought you recently experienced. For the next few minutes, practice accepting the thought and letting it pass on its own. Next, try completing a few tasks that require focus and attention.

3. Did you notice any differences in how long it took you to complete tasks, how many errors you made, and how often your attention drifted away from the task at hand when you were fighting with your intrusive thoughts versus when accepting your intrusive thoughts?

8. Notice Your Change vs. Acceptance Mental Muscles

For the next week, complete this exercise any time you notice your mind activating its change mental muscle versus its acceptance mental muscle.

1. Write the intrusive thought on a small piece of paper.

2. Spend a minute ripping up the piece of paper into tiny pieces. Tell yourself how this thought must go away.

3. Next, write the same thought on a new piece of paper and allow it to rest on your lap.

4. Now decide how you would like to spend the next minute. You can play a game on your phone, answer emails, sit and breathe—anything you want to do.

5. Compare and contrast these experiences of activating your change mental muscle versus your acceptance mental muscle. Which one rattled you, and which one calmed you? Which mental stance allowed you to accomplish more of what *you* would like to spend your time doing, and which left little room to do anything but try to change/eradicate the intrusive thought?

9. Activating Your Acceptance Mental Muscle

Write a recent intrusive thought you have experienced on a small piece of paper. Now, take that piece of paper, crumple it up into a ball, and place it in your shoe. Notice how uncomfortable it is to have this piece of paper poke at your foot. Pay attention to the urge to remove it. Notice how distracting this discomfort is.

Next, practice accepting that the uncomfortable piece of paper is in your shoe, then place your attention on an engaging task such as reading an interesting article, playing with your pet, or watching a TV show. Compare and contrast the experience of railing against the uncomfortable piece of paper in your shoe versus accepting that it is while placing your attention on an engaging activity.

10. A Life Where You Fully Accept ITs

Think about the questions below and write out your answers in a journal or notebook.

- If you had a magic wand and on the count of three—poof!—you are no longer struggling with your intrusive thoughts, how would your life look different?

- What would you be doing right now (besides not reading this book)?

- What activities would you be engaging in?

- What are you missing out on because of your struggles with your intrusive thoughts?

- What is most important to you and how much time in your current life are you spending engaging in activities in line with your top life priorities?

11. Body Scan of Discomfort

Next time you experience an intrusive thought, scan your body and focus on what it feels like to have this uncomfortable thought. The next time you stub your toe or have any other form of physical discomfort, do the same. How are they different? How are they the same? Journal your main takeaways.

12. Assess Discomfort vs. Danger

1. Over the next few days, keep track of any uncomfortable everyday situations that do not bring on feelings of fear or anxiety, like breaking a nail or getting a blister.

2. On a scale of 0 to 10, journal how uncomfortable these sensations are. Jot down how much danger you are in due to this uncomfortable situation, as well as how much anxiety you are experiencing.

3. Over the next few days, track all of your intrusive thoughts. Note the level of discomfort you feel when they surface.

4. Jot down how much danger you are in due to your intrusive thoughts as well as how much anxiety you are experiencing.

Are there any patterns between the ratings for what you've recorded for everyday discomfort and intrusive thought related discomfort? In order to break free from your intrusive thoughts, it's crucial to make the distinction between how uncomfortable an intrusive thought is and how dangerous it is.

13. Notice Your Catastrophic Reactions to Intrusive Thoughts

For the next day, try to notice every time you experience a catastrophic reaction to an intrusive thought. When you notice yourself engaging in an overblown reaction, it's a good time to pull your mind out of its judgmental, catastrophizing spiral and return to the present moment. The 3-3-3 tool (from chapter 5, strategy 6, page 62) is a great method for doing this.

Practice mindfully anchoring yourself in the present moment by naming three things you see, three things you feel, and three things you hear. Once you've interrupted your catastrophic reaction, practice returning your attention to the present. If (and when) catastrophic reactions to an intrusive thought occur, simply notice them and practice coming back to the present again. The more you do this, the fewer and further between your catastrophic reactions will become.

14. Choosing the Acceptance Route

For the next week, any time you experience an intrusive thought:

1. Notice and rate your initial anxiety level (on a scale of 0 to 10).
2. Notice your catastrophic reaction to the intrusive thought.
3. Remind yourself why it is important to accept rather than fight with intrusive thoughts.
4. Practice opening up to the thought and accepting that it has surfaced.
5. Notice and rate your anxiety level (on a scale of 0 to 10) after at least one minute of accepting the thought.

Create a chart to keep track of your findings.

See Tanisha's log below:

DATE/TIME	1/4 4:02 p.m.
REACTION TO INTRUSIVE THOUGHT	I can't keep living like this. How can I be a good teacher if I have such horrific thoughts?
INITIAL ANXIETY LEVEL	9
PROMPT TO PRACTICE ACCEPTING VS. FIGHTING WITH INTRUSIVE THOUGHTS	This thought can't hurt me, but spending endless time fighting with it can hurt me by taking up my time and energy.
POST ACCEPTANCE ANXIETY LEVEL	4

15. Reassess Your Struggle with ITs

For each of these three questions, give an answer from 0 to 10 (0 being the lowest, 10 being the highest), either below or on a separate piece of paper.

How much anxiety and overall emotional distress do you feel about having intrusive thoughts?_____

How often do you avoid certain situations in your life in an effort to avoid intrusive thoughts?_____

How much energy do you spend on an average day trying to extinguish or eradicate your intrusive thoughts?_____

YOUR TOTAL SCORE: [   ]

If you scored from 0 to 14, then the experience of intrusive thoughts is only mildly impairing your ability to live your life to the fullest.

If you scored from 15 to 21, then the experience of intrusive thoughts is moderately impairing your ability to live your life to the fullest.

If you scored from 22 to 30, then the experience of intrusive thoughts is severely impairing your ability to live your life to the fullest.

Compare how you answered each of these questions in this exercise with how you answered these same questions in strategy 1 (page 84). Did you notice any shifts in your score? If your score remained the same, that is okay, too! Creating a new relationship with your intrusive thoughts takes ongoing work and cannot happen instantaneously.

CHAPTER EIGHT

Practice Emotional Regulation

A CRITICAL STEP IN FREEING YOURSELF FROM your intrusive thoughts is learning how to chill out your brain when it is overreacting to them. Learning how to take this emotional reaction down a notch will make it much easier to access the other tools you have learned in this book. With a calm, cool, and collected mind and body, you will be able to swiftly move past intrusive thoughts and invest your energy in living life on your terms.

Your Trigger-Happy Brain

Feeling amped up and overwhelmed is a sign your brain is attempting to manage and organize too much information about potential threats. Like having too many tabs open on your computer or apps running on your phone, trying to manage all of that information at once tends to be inefficient and ineffective, until you need a reboot.

The first step to better navigation of an emotionally charged situation is learning how to calm your body. When you down-regulate, or calm down, your physiology, you will be more effective at problem-solving and distinguishing between true threats and the false alarms generated by intrusive thoughts.

THE MIND-BODY CONNECTION

Your nervous system (NS) is a network of nerves and cells that exchanges information between parts of your body, made up of your sympathetic and your parasympathetic NS. Your sympathetic NS activates your body for "fight or flight" mode, and your parasympathetic NS activates your body for "rest and digest" mode.

When your brain senses you are in danger, it activates your sympathetic NS and turns on all of the bodily functions that assist you in surviving a life-threatening situation, like increasing your oxygen intake and heart rate. The job of your parasympathetic NS is to conserve energy and manage your bodily functions when you are in nonthreatening situations. Your sympathetic and parasympathetic NS together act like the accelerator and brakes on a car. Your sympathetic system is the accelerator that gets you fired up, and your parasympathetic system is the brakes that slow you down.

Activating your parasympathetic NS will send a signal to your brain that you are not in danger. It will then be much easier to see an intrusive thought for what it truly is (brain spam) versus a true threat.

SLOW BREATHING: THE VOLUME DIAL FOR YOUR EMOTIONS

The most powerful and accessible tool you have to calm down your body is your breath. By slowing down, and steadying and decreasing the intensity of your breath, you can activate your parasympathetic (rest and digest) NS. All you need to do to move past an intrusive thought's false alarm signal is engage in 5 minutes of slow breathing. This sends the signal to your brain that there is no need to run and no one to fight, so less oxygen is required to manage this moment.

PROGRESSIVE MUSCLE RELAXATION: THE PRESSURE VALVE FOR YOUR NERVOUS SYSTEM

In addition to using slow breathing to initiate a shift from a state of "fight or flight" to "rest and relaxation," progressive muscle relaxation (PMR) is another simple exercise you can engage in to calm down your nervous system. PMR entails practicing tensing and relaxing all muscles in your body in an exaggerated way.

WHEN THE GOING GETS TOUGH, THERE'S NOTHING WRONG WITH A LITTLE DISTRACTION

Sometimes you are going to feel so flooded with difficult emotions that engaging in the acceptance-based approaches we described in chapter 7 will be unrealistic and too difficult. It is true that the only way past difficult emotions is through them, but there is a time and place for all aspects of functioning, and sometimes the healthiest way to move past an emotionally challenging moment is just to find a way to get through it. Once you have calmed down your brain and body a bit, you can then work your acceptance muscles and practice opening up and riding out the emotional discomfort.

In times of extreme emotional distress, it is never good to sit around thinking about yourself or anyone else, or really to be thinking at all. Thoughts that bubble up in these hot moments will be extreme and inaccurate representations of your true-life situation. These are certainly *not* moments to make any big decisions or take any life-altering actions. The trick in these times is to learn how to focus your attention on anything in the outside world and not on your own extreme thoughts and/or feelings.

DEVELOP A DAILY EMOTION REGULATION PRACTICE

It is important to form a daily practice of engaging in emotional regulation exercises, so we recommend you seek out extra opportunities to practice managing frustrating situations. Yes, you read that correctly. We are encouraging you to make your life slightly more difficult and uncomfortable. It is more difficult to access this tool if you haven't used it in a while, so proactively practicing regulating your emotions will make it much easier to calm yourself down when a frustrating experience occurs. Doing this counterintuitive-sounding work will help your brain build up immunity to emotional discomfort.

The same science behind vaccine effectiveness applies to intentionally exposing yourself to life's small difficulties. A vaccine exposes your body to a small dose of a virus or bacteria. Afterward, your body will use its natural germ-fighting tools to get over the infection. Once your body learns to fight it off, your immune system remembers what it learned about how to protect the body against that disease in the future. Similarly, providing your brain with bite-size emotional distress challenges will help it quickly learn and remember that it can handle these difficult moments instead of battling them.

STRATEGIES AND TECHNIQUES

1. Practice 5 Minutes of Slow Breathing

Set a timer for 5 minutes, then follow these instructions to practice engaging in slow, gentle breathing.

1. Inhale through your nose for 3 seconds, feeling the air gently rise from your belly and slowly make its way to the top of your head.
2. Hold this gentle breath for 3 seconds.
3. Gently release this breath, feeling it slowly leave your mouth for the count of 3.
4. Gently hold your breath for another 3 seconds.
5. Repeat.

2. Take a Breath During Tough Moments

For the next week, log every time you have an anxious or stressed-out moment on your phone or a piece of paper. Record your anxiety level on a scale of 1 to 10 and include a description of what you were doing when these moments showed up, such as running errands or finishing a long workday. Update the rating for your anxiety level after taking 5 minutes to practice slow breathing. How did it change?

3. Label Emotions

Regulating emotions can be as simple as labeling the emotion you are experiencing. Just like how our thoughts do not represent absolute facts about the world, neither do our emotions. By accurately labeling your emotions, you can create distance between you and those emotions, allowing you to think more clearly and decide how to move forward. You will use your body and thoughts to help you determine the emotion you are experiencing.

In this exercise, you will practice bringing awareness to your emotions and labeling them. Watch a TV show or movie and, throughout viewing, use these steps to label your emotions.

1. Notice any of the following changes:

   ▸ Physiological: heart rate, temperature, muscle tension

   ▸ Body language: posture, facial expression, hand gestures

2. Notice your thoughts.

3. Using the information from steps 1 and 2, label the emotions you are experiencing by saying, "I am feeling _____."

When you label your emotions, your brain calms down and over time you learn that you can handle strong emotions instead of shutting them down or having them overwhelm you.

4. **Robot vs. Rag Doll**

1. Tense all the muscles in your body for 15 seconds. Tense your fists. Tense your face. Tense your forehead, eyes and mouth. Tense your shoulders and watch them rise. Tense your stomach. Tense your thighs. Tense your calves. Tense your toes and notice them curl.

2. Next practice releasing all this tension. Imagine you are a rag doll or an overcooked piece of spaghetti. Imagine you are shaking off and releasing all of the excess energy stored in your tense muscles into the universe. Roll your head around a bit, stretch out your mouth, or shake out your hands. Do whatever it takes to feel like you are switching from holding all of your tension in your body to letting go of the tension, releasing it out of your body and into the external world.

3. Repeat three times.

5. Developing Your PMR Muscle Memory

In order to help develop your Progressive Muscle Relaxation (PMR) muscle memory, practice PMR twice a day, once in the morning and once before bed, and track your results. Record how you felt after performing 5 minutes of PMR. See Chloe's log below for an example of how she kept track of this practice.

DAY AND TIME	PRE-PMR ANXIETY LEVEL (0-10)	POST-PMR ANXIETY LEVEL (0-10)	NOTES
9/6: 8:00 a.m.	5	3	I didn't realize how tense my body already was until doing this exercise. I feel better starting my day with less pent-up tension.
9/6: 10:30 p.m.	8	5	During my stressful day, the tension came back. This helped me to release some of the day's stress and relax my mind for sleep.

6. Injecting PMR When in Need of Tension Relief

Just as critical as it is to practice PMR when you are feeling relatively calm in a quiet setting, it is also important to practice applying it to high-stress situations when you could most benefit from this release of tension.

Every time you are in a high-stress situation for the next week, engage in three rounds of PMR. Record how you felt during each situation. Keep track of and note what it is like to inject a little PMR into your highly charged emotional experience. See Chloe's log below for an example of how she began keeping track of this practice.

DAY AND TIME	PRE-PMR ANXIETY LEVEL (0–10)	POST-PMR ANXIETY LEVEL (0–10)	NOTES
9/9 12:00 p.m.	8	5	I'm terrified I'll say something inappropriate during the presentation I'm about to give.
9/12 10:00 p.m.	9	7	I have a huge meeting tomorrow and I'm nowhere near prepared enough. I'm going to have to stay up all night.

7. Change Your Temperature

Changing your body's temperature during an emotionally intense moment can change your mind's channel from the "gloom and doom show" sponsored by your overly revved-up sympathetic NS (fight/flight) to a lighthearted show courtesy of your parasympathetic NS (rest/digest). Keep trying different ideas to change your body's temperature and see what works best for you.

Here are some examples:

- Hold an ice cube
- Go outside and feel the cold breeze, or warm air
- Take a hot or cold shower
- Drink a hot drink or a cold drink

8. Change Your Body Positioning

It is always helpful to change your body positioning from how it was when your initial overwhelming feelings of anxiety set in. For example, if you are sitting hunched over when you notice how stressed you are feeling, stand and stretch by extending your arms up in the air as far as they go. Picture going from a hunched-over turtle to the feathers of a peacock, opening and extending outward.

Other examples of how to change up your body positioning:

- **If you are pacing, sit down**

- **If you feel trapped in your body, do jumping jacks or run the steps in a stairwell**

- **If you are tensing muscles, stand and do a large stretch**

9. Change Your Tactile Experience

This exercise will help you to self-soothe during an extreme moment of emotional distress, shifting your focus onto external things and comforting your tactile senses. Expand the list with more ideas of anything that feels soothing to your touch.

- **Pet your dog, cat, or other pet**

- **Apply lotion and notice how your skin changes from feeling dry to feeling nourished**

- **Play with Silly Putty, slime, or some other fidget toy**

10. Change Your Olfactory Experience

Another way to change your mind's channel from intense emotion to calming relaxation is to soothe yourself through your sense of smell. Using your olfactory experience to evoke a calm and soothing reaction can help comfort you.

- **Carry lavender oil or a lotion with a favorite scent**

- **Use a lip balm with an appealing smell**

11. Offer Yourself a Pleasant and Attention-Grabbing Taste

Keep soothing your senses with a pleasant or unexpected taste. The goal of this emotional regulation exercise is to get your brain engaged in the current moment as quickly as possible, so it can take a break from tending to an extreme (and disproportionate) emotional reaction.

- **Carry mints or gum with you for an on-the-go fix**
- **Chew on small candies that change in taste (sour or tart to sweet)**
- **Reach into your fridge and sample something you have not had in a while (e.g., Dijon mustard, pickles, etc.)**

12. Change the Sound You Are Attending To

Help yourself move past emotionally intense moments with soothing sounds. Paying attention to song lyrics or using your mindfulness skills to focus on a new sound around you can help you refocus from your "stuck" moment and feel soothed by comforting sounds.

- **Create a "Change My Mind's Channel" playlist**
- **Put on your favorite musical, movie soundtrack, or any song that reminds you of a special story**
- **Listen to a song you know every word of so you can sing along**
- **Tune in to a new sound around you and think about the last time (if ever) you really listened to it**

13. Attending to Your Nervous System Through a Quick Body Scan

As you conduct a body scan, it is important to take note of any feelings or sensations that are pulling you away from the present moment. You may instinctively feel the urge to eliminate these sensations, but it's important to simply acknowledge and accept them rather than push them away.

While seated, begin by first bringing your attention to your head. Slowly move from the top of your head down to your shoulders, noticing any feelings of tension or tightness. Then, scan down to your chest and arms, and then through the rest of your torso. Finally, continue to move down your body and notice the feeling of contact between your legs and your seat, and then to how your feet make contact with the floor.

14. Develop an Ongoing Practice
For the next week, when you are in an enjoyable or neutral situation and feel relatively calm, take a moment to pay attention to your body and engage in the body scan exercise described above. If you notice any excess tension, spend a minute doing progressive muscle relaxation or slow breathing.

15. Work Your Emotional Regulation Muscle Daily
Identify one mildly frustrating task that you need to engage in each day. Before you complete the task, decide which emotional regulation strategy you are going to use if you notice your sympathetic NS running the show, causing you to feel a disproportionate and extreme stress reaction.

Compare and contrast your distress level from before you engaged in the emotional regulation exercise and after. Was it higher or lower overall? Did you notice any patterns? Were there some challenges that were easier for you to downregulate extreme emotions versus others?

CHAPTER NINE

Live Your Best Life

THINK ABOUT YOUR LIFE RIGHT NOW.
Is it run by you or your ITs? This chapter will
assist you in living your best life, even with
the occasional IT. You will learn strategies to
put the things that are important to you and
the life you want to be living into perspective.
Your values are key and help to revitalize you
and keep you moving forward toward meaningful
life experiences. This chapter will help you be
guided by your values instead of letting your
ITs hijack all of your time and energy.

What Does Your Best Life Look Like?

Think back to your answer to the magic wand question in chapter 7, strategy 10 (page 89). What came to mind when you thought about a life without ITs? Now, think about your life and notice if there is anything that helps you better access your best life. If you can't see these answers clearly yet, you are at the right place. There is no right or wrong way to live your best life.

Living your best life is about living a life full of *your* values. Continuous exploration of what works for you and doesn't, what is important to you and isn't, provides you with perspective, so you can focus on your life instead of being consumed by unwanted thoughts. Valued living also involves acknowledgment of and appreciation for your own strengths and unique characteristics.

YOUR BEST LIFE DOES NOT EQUAL EVERLASTING HAPPINESS

People almost always list happiness as an ultimate life goal. We are here to tell you that being happy does not equate to living your best life. A common misconception of happiness is that life is "good" when you feel happy and "bad" when you don't. This is thankfully not true. Happiness is an emotion, and it comes and goes like all feelings. When you think about your best life, instead of focusing on how you want to feel—since your feelings will continually change!—we challenge you to strive for fulfillment.

FINDING FULFILLMENT WITH VALUES

Feeling fulfilled means energizing yourself both physically and emotionally by moving toward the things that are important to you. Values provide direction and guidance and help get you invested in moving forward with activities that fulfill you. Incorporating your values into daily life can enhance motivation and increase your brain's flexibility to move through old patterns of resistance and avoidance. They make getting through the tough stuff worth it. In fact, when you act according to your values, research shows that it can help you to feel more satisfied in your life, beyond just feeling less anxious.

COMMIT TO YOUR VALUES

It is important to identify your values and equally essential to commit to them. Committing to values means engaging in activities or tasks that align with them and incorporating them into your daily life. It doesn't matter if your values-based action takes 2 minutes or 2 hours, as long as you carve out time for the things you love and take action toward the things you want, instead of waiting for the "perfect timing" or until you feel the "right amount" of motivation. Keep a routine or set a schedule to ensure you keep moving in the direction of your values.

MAKING ROOM FOR ITS IN YOUR BEST LIFE

Your ITs will accompany you as you live your best life. You will move toward the important things, knowing that your ITs may call for your attention. Your job is to acknowledge them and your feelings, without validating their content (like a child throwing a temper tantrum), then refocus on the task of serving your values. The ITs are there and we can't make them go away, but we can divert our attention to the things that matter most. Willingness to move forward with your values, despite any discomfort that may show up, will be essential. Soon enough, you will see that the more you can devote your mental energy and efforts to the things you love, your annoying ITs will lose all power they once had over you. They will still make some guest appearances, but they won't have the leading role in your life story.

STRATEGIES AND TECHNIQUES

1. Who's Calling the Shots?

When your life feels consumed by your ITs, it's important to get an idea of what is your "sweet spot" of living life. Although we cannot get rid of ITs, we can strive to have them become background noise instead of guiding your moves every which way. Let's get some perspective on how your life operates right now.

On a piece of paper, create a pie chart by logging the percentages of 1) how much you actively control and live your valued life and 2) how much of your life is controlled by your ITs. On the other side of this piece of paper, create another pie chart, but this time assign percentages to where you realistically want those numbers to be in the future. Remember, you can't assign a zero to ITs, as they will continue to be part of your life, but they certainly don't have to be leading it.

Set a reminder on your phone or calendar for three months from now. Reapproach this strategy with curiosity. Were there any changes in your ratings? What do you think has happened in the past few months that led to these differences or kept them the same? Is your life led by *you* or by your ITs?

2. Shine a Spotlight on Your ITs

Think about where your ITs are appearing and impacting you in various areas of your life. On a separate piece of paper, file your ITs under different categories, such as friendships, romantic relationships, and work. Try to include as many categories as you can. Then write down and describe the impact that your ITs have on each category. How could each category of your life look different if the influence of your ITs was reduced?

3. Fears vs. Values

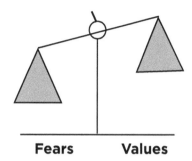

Fears   **Values**

Think about a balance scale like the one here. On one side, you have your ITs' fears influencing an action (*I won't go on a roof-top patio in case I lose control and jump*). On the other side, you have your own preferences and values (*I will go on the rooftop because I love watching sunsets*). Make a list of all the things your ITs tell you to do; label this side "Fear." On the other side, make a list of all the things your values would like you to do; label this side "Values."

Reflect on which actions you tend to take: the ones fueled by fear and pushed by your ITs' agenda, or the ones based on your preferences and crafted in service of your values?

Notice any "shoulds" or "rules" pushed forward by your ITs. Which side are they on? Notice which actions feel authentic to who you are. Which side are those on?

For the next week, use this balance scale when making important decisions. Ask yourself: *Am I making this decision based on my fears (ITs) or my values (preferences)?* Note that both might be there, but the goal is for your values to lead the way.

4. Who and What Are Important to You?

Without thinking too hard about it, jot down five things that are important to you. We are going to expand on this in a search for your top values. Now conduct an Internet search for a "values list." You can find websites and images with an expansive listing of core values. Here is your task:

1. **Read through the list and write down all the values that are important to you. Don't spend too much time here. Avoid choosing values that feel like they should be important to you and focus on the values that feel authentic to you.**

2. Narrow your chosen values to your Top 10 Values.

3. Now, narrow it further down to your Top 5 Values.

4. Beside each value, write down what it means to you.

5. For each value, on a scale from 0 to 5, rate how consistent this value is in your life (0 = distant, 5 = consistent).

Was there anything surprising about your Top 5 Values? Take a moment to reflect on how these values show up (or have not yet shown up) within your different life domains (see strategy 2 on page 110 for ideas).

5. Opposite Values

Use humor to defuse the discomfort and uncertainty that ITs cause for you. Make a list of your opposite values: things that you can absolutely identify as unimportant to you or find ridiculously silly. Notice your reaction when you say your opposite values aloud. Does it make you question your values? Does it sound so outlandish that you laugh and can better see your actual values? Beside each opposite value on the list, write down a connection to one of your true values.

6. And the Award Goes to . . .

Imagine you have just won a prestigious lifetime achievement award. Take a moment to sit in this excitement, discomfort, or whatever comes up for you. Your task is to write the script for the person that honors you with the award. Talk about past experiences, current circumstances, and aspirational goals and values you would hope to be recognized for in the future. Notice when your doubting thoughts appear and try to inject some compassionate ones to take their place. Remember, you are being admired for your unique journey through life.

Here are some ideas to get you started:

  - **Which memorable moments will you highlight?**
  - **Which challenging obstacles have you faced?**

- Were there any changes in your life that helped you to move forward?
- Who was there along the way (family, friends, coworkers, mentors)?
- Who or what inspired you to accomplish all that you have?
- Have you influenced or been a mentor to others?

7. Values Action Plan

Come back to your (true) Top 5 Values. For each value, find three activities or tasks that are consistent with what that value means to you. Each week, focus on incorporating a specific value into your routine, whether it is 2 minutes or 2 hours long. Don't spend too long planning; there is no right or wrong way to engage in a values-based activity if it feels like it matters to you. See fellow traveler Chloe's (page 11) start to this exercise:

TOP 5 VALUES	COMMITTED ACTION PLAN
Connection	1. Share a post on social media. 2. Call my mom. 3. Text an old friend.
Creativity	1. Use my watercolors to paint. 2. Search for local clubs or groups to meet other creative people. 3. Write the first few sentences of a short story.

8. What Roadblocks Lie Ahead?

Now that you have an action plan for living in your values, it's important to plan for roadblocks your ITs may throw in your path to disrupt your valued living. Get the upper hand so that you can flexibly continue with your commitment to your values action plan, despite any sabotage from ITs.

Using the chart example, think of potential roadblocks to the Top 5 Values and committed actions you identified in the previous exercises. Here are Chloe's potential roadblocks and her plan to flexibly detour around them:

COMMITTED ACTIONS (VALUE)	POTENTIAL ROADBLOCK	DETOUR ROUTE
Share a post on social media. (Connection)	I might feel embarrassed and not do it.	I can pick a lighthearted topic to share with my friends. Maybe something funny or heartwarming.
Call my mom. (Connection)	I will tell myself I am too busy for our usual 30-minute calls.	I can text my mom before I call her telling her I have a full day ahead of me, but that I would like to chat for 10 minutes today.

9. You're Dead; Now What?

We are going to pretend that your life has been lived to the fullest and that you are no longer with us. Morbid, right? Now imagine that you are at your grave looking at your tombstone, but there is no inscription yet. What would you write on it? How would you want to be remembered? What would you want the world to know about your life?

You can start with: "Here lies [your name]. They lived a life full of . . ." How does that feel to say? Which values showed up for you?

Now, imagine your life exactly as it is now. And you find yourself no longer living and again you are at your blank tombstone. The inscription will represent what you have stood for in your life so far and what you have made a priority through your actions. What would this tombstone say now?

Recognize if different reactions show up for you as you reflect on both tombstones. What, if anything, could you do differently with your time and effort as you live out your life? How could you make room for the meaningful things instead of the things that take up most of your attention right now?

10. Sorting for Values

In the flurry of ITs that run through our mind, it is sometimes hard to tell what is important and what is brain spam. Here is a list of thoughts that you are to sort as either brain spam (ITs, or things that don't matter) or priority mail (things that matter).

Random Brain Thoughts:

What if I'm hungry later?

The wind feels so nice on my face.

What if I am so hungry, I start eating uncontrollably?

The wind may push me into a total stranger.

I am feeling turned on after that movie. Where is my partner?

I must be a thief if I tried a grape in the grocery store.

Why did watching a sex scene in a movie about high schoolers make me feel aroused?

I should use this knife carefully as I slice up some watermelon.

Should I sample some fruit at the grocery store?

11. Zooming Out for Perspective

It can be helpful to gain some big-picture perspective during times we feel so stuck that all we can see is the deep dark hole of our problem and every IT that goes along with it. When we "zoom out," we can also see all the other integral parts of our life at play.

1. Think about a time your ITs got you feeling really stuck. Ask yourself: Will this issue matter in 10 minutes (probably), 10 weeks (maybe), 10 months (we'll see), or 10 years (possibly)? Sit with the uncertainty while acknowledging the realistic likelihood of your specific issue at hand mattering at each time increment.
2. Think about your values. Ask yourself: Will my values matter in 10 minutes (yes), 10 weeks (yes), 10 months (maybe/yes), 10 years (hopefully yes)? Here, we learn that values will also matter, because they are by definition the things that are most important to you. While the content may change over time, your values will always be with you as you move along in life.

12. Willingness in Service of Your Values

We can't control our feelings of discomfort, but we can pour our efforts into our willingness to act. Willingness is the mechanism that can help you move toward your values, even with the discomfort brought on by your ITs. Watch out for the inaccurate rule your mind may offer: *If you feel any discomfort, you are not willing to do it.*

Look back at your values action plan you created in strategy 7 (page 113). Beside each committed action plan entry, write down two numbers from 0 to 10 (0 being the lowest, 10 being the highest) that represent 1) your level of discomfort, and 2) your level of willingness to engage in the action. Notice any patterns you see with these two ratings. Can you challenge yourself to move forward in service of your values, using willingness as a guide instead of your anxiety?

13. Offering Thanks to Yourself and Others

Feeling grateful has many benefits. Practicing gratitude can help increase empathy, improve mental and physical health, enhance self-esteem, and encourage more social connection.

Use the following prompts to explore your appreciation for the things around you.

I am grateful for two things I see/hear/smell/taste/feel:

I am grateful for these two friends/family members:

I am grateful for these two things at work/school/home:

I am grateful for these two skills of mine:

14. Flexibly Moving Through Unfulfilling Moments
Map out your go-to tools for sitting through life's naturally unfulfilling moments. Set up your SOS plan for unfulfilling moments (like extra work piled on you by your boss or arguing with family members) by completing this checklist to remind yourself that you have got this! Refer back to this checklist or make one on your own that you can reference when it is hard to see past your ITs to your path of valued living.

Check Yourself:

What are my strengths?

What is a helpful way to think about my IT?

What is something kind I can say to myself?

What actions *will* work for me and are aligned with my values?

Reflect:

Are there rules stuck in my head for how I "should" be acting?

Are my ITs sabotaging my path to valued living?

> Which of my values are tied to the specific task
> I have at hand?

15. Set Yourself Up for Fulfillment

Put it all together and set yourself up for leading a fulfilling and meaningful life. Here are some tips to keep you moving forward and committed to your values:

> **Keep your values in sight.**

> **Zoom out and open yourself up to new perspectives.**

> **Be flexible through tough moments.**

> **Keep a routine and schedule in daily doses of values-based actions.**

> **Use a tracking chart or engage in actions with a friend to keep yourself accountable.**

> **Reward yourself for following through and making time for the important things.**

CHAPTER TEN

Grow Bored of Your Intrusive Thoughts

BELIEVE IT OR NOT, IT IS POSSIBLE TO GROW bored of even the most offensive, attention-grabbing IT. The human brain is primed to seek out and attempt to make sense of new information for survival purposes, so it has an amazing ability—known as habituation—to grow bored of any stimulus after repeated exposure to it. Our brain also has the amazing ability to continually learn and adapt, making new neural connections and memory road maps each time we do something new. This chapter will provide you with the "secret sauce" of effective treatment for intrusive thoughts: habituation and learning through repeated exposure to fear-inducing stimuli.

Habituation, Learning, and You

Habituation to and learning from a fear-inducing, uncomfortable stimulus may sound like a new concept, but we guarantee it is a phenomenon you have experienced countless times in your life. Any time you started out having a strong emotional reaction to a stimulus and eventually felt a minimal emotional reaction to it, by definition, you have habituated to that stimulus through repeated exposure to it.

When introduced to the concept of habituation, Chloe (page 11) struggled to grasp its application to her own life. She could buy into the relevance of habituation to her goal of breaking free from ITs after reviewing prior instances when she shifted from fearing something to feeling neutral about it.

If Chloe found a parking spot that required parallel parking, she would drive around until she found a larger spot. She was therefore often late and caught in the rain. One day she grew frustrated enough with her fear, avoidance of parallel parking, and the negative impact on her life that she decided to just go for it. Attempting to back into a spot, all she could see in her rearview mirror was an annoyed driver's face behind her, waiting for her to move. She began to panic and felt her heart rate increasing, but somehow found the strength to push forward and face her fear. The next few times Chloe had to parallel park were uncomfortable, but she noticed an internal shift. Soon enough, with repeated practice (exposure) she no longer experienced an extreme emotional reaction (habituation) and she knew she could tolerate the discomfort if it did show up again (learning) when needing to parallel park. She never thought she could grow bored of an act that she had so recently found terrifying and worthy of avoiding at all costs.

SHORT-TERM PAIN, LONG-TERM GAIN

As practitioners, we are big fans of the "rip off the Band-Aid fast" method and believers in a bit of short-term pain for a whole lot of long-term gain. That is exactly what the powerful tool of exposure is going to provide you with—a lifetime of long-term gain in the form of freedom from your ITs.

Say you want to start swimming regularly to get into better shape, but the water feels uncomfortably cold when you lower your body into the pool. You could retreat from the water, wrap up in a warm towel, and read a book instead of working out. You'll probably feel better in the moment, but you won't get any healthier physically. The other option is to jump in, facing the initial shock of cold water but quickly becoming acclimated as you swim, working toward your goal of getting into better shape.

CONGRATULATIONS!

If you are finding that reading this book is occasionally anxiety provoking because you have encountered different trigger words, congratulate yourself for completing exposure exercises. Tolerating the discomfort that these words may have elicited takes you one step closer to freeing yourself from ITs.

CREATE YOUR OWN EXPOSURE PLAN

Breaking free from your ITs includes experientially teaching your brain that they are momentarily uncomfortable but not dangerous, like the first few moments you jump into a cold pool. The first step of engaging in exposure to IT exercises is to clearly identify all current as well as any prior ITs that still elicit a strong and disproportionate emotional reaction.

DEVELOP A ROUTINE

Much like lifting weights at the gym, routinely exposing yourself to an intrusive thought makes you stronger and takes power away from these thoughts.

The way to get your brain to habituate to your ITs, or to grow bored of and properly identify them as brain spam, is to engage in exposure exercises daily for at least 30 minutes a day, until your anxiety rating for each thought decreases by half or more. To maximize results, we recommend breaking up your exposure workout session to twice daily, 15 minutes each practice period, and to do this in different settings, like your car or at a coffee shop. We need to get your brain to comprehend these thoughts as uncomfortable, but not dangerous.

THE TYPES OF EXPOSURES
Here are examples of five different exposure techniques:

Visual Exposures
- Reading trigger words associated with an IT repeatedly for at least 2 minutes, or until anxiety level drops by half or more.
- Writing out a scary story associated with an IT and reading it repeatedly for at least 2 minutes, or until anxiety level drops by half or more.
- Watching a video clip associated with an IT repeatedly for at least 2 minutes, or until anxiety level drops by half or more.

Auditory Exposure
- Saying trigger words out loud repeatedly for at least 2 minutes, or until anxiety level drops by half or more.
- Creating an audio file of a "scary story" associated with an IT, then listening to it on repeat for at least 2 minutes, or until anxiety level drops by half or more.

Proprioceptive Exposures
- Engaging in a physical motion associated with an IT repeatedly for at least 2 minutes, or until anxiety level drops by half or more.

In Vivo Exposures

- Exposing yourself to any situation or environment you are currently avoiding for fear it will bring on the IT or that you will lose control and engage in feared behavior and spend time in that environment (without engaging in any safety behaviors or compulsions) until anxiety level drops by at least half.

Interoceptive Exposures

- Interoceptive exposures bring on the sensations associated with feeling anxious to train your brain that the feelings of anxiety are uncomfortable but not dangerous (e.g., breathing through a straw to simulate the sensation of having trouble breathing). Your brain can learn it may not like feeling anxious and out of control, but it can handle these sensations.

HABITUATION AND LEARNING WILL OCCUR ACROSS EXPOSURES

Clients often feel it will be a game of Whack-A-Mole, their brain simply replacing one IT with a new one. The good news is that with each exposure, the intensity of the next IT to surface and the work required to move past it will be much less. In addition, the frequency of ITs surfacing will decrease. This is because your brain will no longer be on high alert, fearing when the next thought will surface, which you now know is the most effective way to summon an IT. You will find as you move through your exposure hierarchy that many items naturally drop off, and no longer elicit anxiety. We recommend making contact with each item on your hierarchy; if you note that your anxiety in reaction to this thought is low or nonexistent, there is no need to conduct any direct exposures with this IT.

The exact exposures that will work for you will be somewhat different than the exposures that would be most effective for someone else struggling with the same IT. However, the key ingredients of a high-quality exposure will always be the same: repeatedly making mental contact with the most anxiety-inducing aspects of an intrusive thought without interruption or distraction, or letting yourself engage in any mental compulsions to avoid contact with the IT.

The more contact your brain has with the IT, the more efficiently and effectively it learns to identify it as brain spam vs. critical messaging.

STRATEGIES AND TECHNIQUES

1. Let's Practice Habituating

As discussed above, all feelings and reactions shift and diminish over time, with repeated exposure to novel stimuli.

1. Find a scented lotion or candle (or anything else with a noteworthy scent, such as a food item).

2. Place the scented item under your nose and smell it for a few moments, then put it down. On a 0 to 10 scale, note how strong the scent was (with 0 being not at all and 10 being an extremely noteworthy scent).

3. Next, place the scented object under your nose and keep it there for 1 minute. Whenever your attention wanders off to a different stimulus, gently bring it back to the scent you are mindfully attending to.

4. After 1 minute of mindfully attending to the scent, note the strength of the scent (using the 0 to 10 scale, with 0 being not at all and 10 being an extremely noteworthy scent).

2. Reviewing Beliefs or Preconceived Notions About Engaging in Exposures

Many clients have come to us for treatment for intrusive thoughts after researching the topic on their own, in an attempt to make sense of and to figure out how to combat these thoughts. As part of this research, they find literature, websites, or television programming that introduce the concept of exposure-based therapy and provide examples. Making contact with this material can sometimes be helpful, as they assist in shedding light on a painful and confusing aspect of your life. However, reviewing treatment material can sometimes lead to a new form of anticipatory anxiety where you may come to the conclusion, *If freedom from intrusive thoughts requires doing all of these scary exposures, then progress will be hopeless because I will never get myself to do these kinds of things*. We work with our clients to understand that we will be taking baby steps to move forward with exposures and that they will never be pushed beyond what they can handle. You can't break or lose it if you push yourself too hard. The worst that will happen is you will end up not doing an exposure because it feels too difficult, and then you will not make the progress you are hoping for.

Spend a few minutes identifying and listing any preconceived notions you may have about exposure-based exercises in relation to your ITs. Next, let's apply the cognitive reframing you have learned about in chapter 6 (strategy 11, page 78) to provide yourself with a more realistic perspective on just how scary or overwhelming it will be to engage in exposure exercises.

See Lucas's (page 11) example:

FEARS REGARDING EXPOSURE-BASED EXERCISES	REALISTIC COUNTERPOINTS REGARDING EXPOSURE-BASED EXERCISES
I won't be able to handle them.	I might not like it, but my head won't explode. One way or another, I will get through them.
I will have to do so many scary things at once.	I can pace myself and take small steps forward.
Doing an exposure may cause me to act out my feared behavior.	I have already had the feared thought more times than I can count, and I still have not engaged in my feared behavior.

3. Expose Yourself to Strong Reactions

Find an article or image online that brings up an intense emotional response. Think about controversial or taboo topics, such as politics, climate change, current events in the news, gun violence, human trafficking, or anything else that evokes a strong emotional reaction. Take note of your initial level of emotional reaction. Now, continue to view or reread the article or image until your level of emotional reaction decreases.

Note that you may always have some level of discomfort when you view or encounter certain topics, but with exposure (e.g., rereading articles), your emotional reaction will probably not be as strong as the first time you encountered them. Maybe you even grew bored of reading about the news! The idea is that once you have habituated to the content of the topic, it doesn't evoke that same strong response it did at first.

4. Expose Yourself to "Scary" Words

Review the following list, and on a scale from 0 to 10 rate how anxious each word or phrase makes you.

Losing control	Never knowing
Psychopath	Deranged
Murder	Devil
Suicide	Pervert
Pedophile	Insane

For any word you rated greater than 0 in eliciting anxiety, say the word 100 times out loud. Note how anxious you are feeling before you do the exposure exercise and how anxious you feel after.

5. Acceptance-Based Exposure Work

Take a moment to practice bringing on an intrusive thought. Then allow yourself to engage in some kind of compulsion to bring down your anxiety level, provide yourself with some relief, and reassure yourself that you are okay.

Next, bring on an intrusive thought with an open, accepting posture and allow yourself to feel and move through all of the sensations, feelings, and discomfort that surface.

Now compare and contrast these two experiences. Which experience brought on more immediate discomfort? Which experience brought on short-term relief? What can you take away in regard to how to get the most out of your exposure exercises?

6. Create an Exposure Hierarchy

Take a few moments to list all the ITs you fear, the behaviors you engage in to avoid or neutralize these thoughts, and your current level of anxiety when confronted by these thoughts.

See the start of Chloe's chart:

INTRUSIVE THOUGHT	AVOIDANCE/SAFETY/ NEUTRALIZING BEHAVIORS/ COMPULSIONS	ANXIETY LEVEL WHEN CONFRONTED BY INTRUSIVE THOUGHT (0–10)
Losing control and killing self	Hide knives Avoid high spots where I could leap to death Lock up all sharp objects at night Obtain reassurance from my mother that I would never do this Read articles about people who have lost control and killed themselves and compare with my own experience If I have the thought, *I am going to lose control and kill myself*, list out all the reasons I have to live and remind myself that I would never do that	10
Losing control and stabbing boyfriend	Hide knives Lock up all sharp objects at night Obtain reassurance from my mother that I would never do this Read articles about the difference between OCD and being a psychopath, and compare with my own experience	10

continued ▶

INTRUSIVE THOUGHT	AVOIDANCE/SAFETY/ NEUTRALIZING BEHAVIORS/ COMPULSIONS	ANXIETY LEVEL WHEN CONFRONTED BY INTRUSIVE THOUGHT (0–10)
Going crazy and yelling out obscenities	Give myself mental quizzes to make sure I still have mental faculties Close mouth super tight to make sure no strange, disturbing words come out of my mouth unintentionally Review prior conversations to determine if by accident I said something inappropriate Call friends and coworkers to assess if they are acting differently to me because I said something inappropriate	8

7. Identifying Your Exposures

For one of the top ITs you identified in the previous strategy as triggering, identify exposures you can engage in that provide your brain with full sensory contact with the thought through visual, auditory, proprioceptive, and interoceptive pathways.

See Chloe's exposure plan:

INTRUSIVE THOUGHT	SAMPLE EXPOSURE EXERCISES
Losing control and stabbing boyfriend	**Visual Exposure:** Watch a TV show or movie with stabbing.
Losing control and stabbing boyfriend	**Auditory Exposure:** Record and listen to audio recording of a story of killing one's boyfriend.

INTRUSIVE THOUGHT	SAMPLE EXPOSURE EXERCISES
Losing control and stabbing boyfriend	**Proprioceptive Exposure:** Cut into meat imagining it is one's boyfriend.
Losing control and stabbing boyfriend	**In Vivo Exposure:** Chop food while boyfriend is in the kitchen.
Losing control and stabbing boyfriend	**Interoceptive Exposures:** Spin around really fast, then go stand by or sit next to boyfriend.

8. Confront What You've Been Avoiding

Write down a list of trigger words and images related to your intrusive thoughts. Include anything that you avoid on purpose, such as specific words, phrases, or images. For Chloe, her avoided triggers included the word "pedophile," the phrase "that is perverted," the words "criminally insane," and images of prison.

Throughout the week, your job is to purposefully expose yourself to the words and images that bother you. Stare at each one separately and see how long you can keep viewing it over and over. Even when your mind tells you to look away, see if you can keep looking for 10 more seconds. Track your pre-exposure level of anxiety and your postexposure level of anxiety (both on a scale from 0 to 10). How long does it take for your anxiety to come down by half? Was it longer, shorter, or just as you had expected?

Now, repeat this exercise, but try saying these words or describing the images out loud. Then repeat this exercise again, but try writing these words or drawing the images on a piece of paper.

Be sure to track your pre- and postexposure levels of anxiety so that your brain can soak up the benefits and learn from your hard work engaging in these exposures.

9. Creating Your Own Exposure Exercises

For each of the ITs you identified in strategy 6, design an exposure exercise accessing each of the sensory pathways reviewed in the previous section. We have provided a sample chart that you can use when creating your exposure plan.

INTRUSIVE THOUGHT	SAMPLE EXPOSURE EXERCISES	PRE-EXPOSURE ANXIETY RATING (0–10)	POSTEXPOSURE ANXIETY RATING (0–10)
Intrusive Thought 1	**Visual Exposure**		
Intrusive Thought 1	**Auditory Exposure**		
Intrusive Thought 1	**Proprioceptive Exposure**		
Intrusive Thought 1	**In Vivo Exposure**		
Intrusive Thought 1	**Interoceptive Exposures**		
Intrusive Thought 2	**Visual Exposure**		
Intrusive Thought 2	**Auditory Exposure**		
Intrusive Thought 2	**Proprioceptive Exposure**		
Intrusive Thought 2	**In Vivo Exposure**		

INTRUSIVE THOUGHT	SAMPLE EXPOSURE EXERCISES	PRE-EXPOSURE ANXIETY RATING (0–10)	POSTEXPOSURE ANXIETY RATING (0–10)
Intrusive Thought 2	**Interoceptive Exposures**		
Intrusive Thought 3	**Visual Exposure**		
Intrusive Thought 3	**Auditory Exposure**		
Intrusive Thought 3	**Proprioceptive Exposure**		
Intrusive Thought 3	**In Vivo Exposure**		
Intrusive Thought 3	**Interoceptive Exposures**		

10. No Need to Go It Alone

To obtain the most long-lasting results from all of the hard work you have already invested in obtaining freedom from ITs, it is best to enlist a trusted friend, family member, or therapist you can rely on to serve as your "intrusive thought exposure coach." Even if your identified exposure coach plays a minimal role in the actual treatment plan, it is still healing to discuss your symptoms with a loved one. It will be a hard but powerful first step forward. It will help to confirm there is nothing wrong with you as you navigate through some scary thoughts that you are struggling to make sense of.

11. Staying Motivated and Held Accountable

Identify what motivates you to do this difficult but important work of breaking free from your intrusive thoughts. (Hint: What do you value the most? What areas of your life are you no longer willing to sacrifice in order to avoid contact with intrusive thoughts?)

Review all of your exposure assignments with the coach you identified in strategy 10. Brainstorm a list of ways to be held accountable for the tasks you set for yourself, which can include any of the following:

- **Include friends or family to join your exposure practice.**

- **Keep a daily exposure practice log.**

- **Schedule a weekly check-in time with your coach, or check in with yourself by doing some journaling.**

- **Display sticky notes with reminders or motivational messages in places you'll see throughout the day (such as your bathroom mirror or desk).**

When you lose sight of the harm caused by buying into your intrusive thoughts and what you potentially have to gain when you face ITs head-on, check in with your coach or therapist. They can remind you of your motivation to do this difficult work.

12. Exposures and Response Prevention

When experiencing moderate to severe discomfort in relation to intrusive thoughts, we recommend creating a daily or twice-a-day schedule of exposing yourself intentionally and actively to your ITs. But when these thoughts come up on their own during a time outside of the practice period, and when you may be engaging in alternate, value-driven behavior, we recommend simply tapping into response prevention and then mindfully redirecting yourself back to the current moment.

For example, say you were having dinner with your family when you suddenly have the thought, *What if I lose control and stab myself with a knife?* At this juncture you have a few options:

Option 1: Engage in a compulsion and move the knife away from yourself and follow up with mental compulsions such as praying or reminding yourself that you would never take your own life. Remind yourself of the checklist qualities of people who kill themselves and that you do not meet the criteria.

Option 2: Engage in an exposure to the thought and take a moment to think in a repetitive fashion, *I am going to stab myself.* Then write this thought down 30 times in a row.

Option 3: You can choose to simply engage in response prevention, meaning not giving in to your urge to engage in your compulsions, and instead tell yourself, *I can't promise I am not going to lose control and stab myself, but what I can do is return back to the current moment and place my attention back on the aspects of life that are most important to me.*

For the next week, outside of your daily exposure practice period, practice response prevention by engaging in these four steps:

1. **Notice when an intrusive thought surfaces.**
2. **Notice the urge to engage in different compulsions or safety behaviors to manage the anxiety you are experiencing.**
3. **Choose to not give in to the urge to engage in a compulsion.**
4. **Actively return your attention to the present moment (rather than give in to the urge to do the compulsion).**

13. Beating Your Intrusive Thoughts to the Punch

At some point in the future, a new intrusive thought will surface. So, let's get ahead of your ITs by considering some new material your brain may throw your way.

Review the most common categories of ITs on page 7 and for each category think of one potential thought your brain could present to you in the future. Record your anxiety level when exposing yourself to these sample intrusive thoughts.

14. Play the Opposite Game with Your ITs

Dealing with ITs is like a never-ending opposite game. The most effective, healing move when confronted by an IT is to do the opposite of what it demands of you.

For the next week, every time you experience an IT keep a log of the following:

1. Describe the intrusive thought.
2. What compulsion/safety behavior are you feeling the urge to do in response to the IT?
3. How can you play the opposite game with this IT? What is one exposure you can engage in to teach your brain it need not take seriously nor fear this thought?

15. Start with One Exposure Every Day

As our clients start making progress in decreasing the frequency and intensity of their intrusive thoughts, eventually they will experience a very long time period when no intrusive thoughts surface. The one downside of a quiet, IT-free period of life is that your brain forgets what to do when it eventually makes contact with one. Your brain once again can come to believe that a scary thought is equivalent to a scary action.

In order to keep this key concept fresh and top of mind, it is important to engage in an intrusive thought exposure exercise on a daily basis. Actively bring on one intrusive, scary thought and then let any uncomfortable feelings pass on their own. Similar to setting up good oral hygiene routines of brushing and flossing on a daily basis, it should become second nature to pick a consistent time every day to do a mini one-minute IT exposure exercise.

Thoughts for Going Forward

REFLECT ON HOW FAR YOU HAVE COME SINCE learning about and engaging with your ITs through these exercises. Think about how daunting and distant any progress initially seemed. You are over the most difficult part: confronting your ITs and intentionally spending more time with them as you have done throughout this book. Sit with this win for a moment and acknowledge all your hard work and commitment for making it this far. Go you!

Progress may not feel linear; there will be bumps in the road, expected and unexpected life stressors, and inevitable dips in mood that might make you feel like you are back at square one. Don't be discouraged or surprised by these bumps. When you do hit an obstacle, be gentle with yourself and keep moving forward. This is an especially powerful time to enhance your skills by giving them extra attention and practice.

The good news is that it is impossible for you to be back at the beginning of this process. You will still be on that upward, linear trend of progress. At the beginning you did not have the knowledge, tools, or experience that you have now acquired through this book. So, unless you skipped ahead to the conclusion without reading a single chapter, congratulations! You have made progress.

The next step is to keep the momentum going. You may be sick of thinking about your ITs. But continual work on your ITs can stop them from gaining influence over your life again. Write a note or find an IT-fighting mantra that speaks to you, reminding you why it is important to move through instead of avoiding your feelings of discomfort. Just as you have done with each chapter, it is important to remain systematic and consistent in engaging your ITs. With each exercise you do, you strengthen your new skills that keep ITs in their place—and out of your space.

Here are some tips to keep you moving forward:
1. Identify the tools and techniques from each chapter that you value most.
2. Recognize the warning signs that let you know when it's time to use your tools.
3. Try different tools to see what works best for you.
4. Schedule some check-ins with yourself. Life gets busy, so dedicate time every few weeks to see what is or is not working for you and make the appropriate adjustments to your IT-busting toolbox.
5. Connect, connect, and connect with your values. Move toward the things that are important to you to reclaim fulfillment in *your* life, instead of fulfilling your ITs' demands.

Intrusive thoughts are intermittent, but you have the strength to manage them. Think of what advice you would offer to others struggling with ITs and give yourself that same compassionate guidance. You deserve a full, rich, and meaningful life, with or without ITs.

We know you can do this.

Resources

BOOKS

Overcoming Unwanted Intrusive Thoughts: A CBT-Based Guide to Getting Over Frightening, Obsessive, or Disturbing Thoughts by Sally M. Winston and Martin N. Seif (2017)

Needing to Know for Sure: A CBT-Based Guide to Overcoming Compulsive Checking and Reassurance Seeking by Martin N. Seif and Sally M. Winston (2019)

Rewire Your Anxious Brain: How to Use the Neuroscience of Fear to End Anxiety, Panic, and Worry by Catherine M. Pittman and Elizabeth M Karle (2015)

The Happiness Trap: How to Stop Struggling and Start Living: A Guide to ACT by Russ Harris (2008)

A Liberated Mind: How to Pivot Toward What Matters by Steven C. Hayes (2019)

Everyday Mindfulness for OCD: Tips, Tricks, and Skills for Living Joyfully by Jon Hershfield and Shala Nicely (2017)

The Worry Trick: How Your Brain Tricks You into Expecting the Worst and What You Can Do About It by David A. Carbonell (2006)

When a Family Member Has OCD: Mindfulness and Cognitive Behavioral Skills to Help Families Affected by Obsessive-Compulsive Disorder by Jon Hershfield (2015)

WORKBOOKS

The CBT Anxiety Solution Workbook: A Breakthrough Treatment for Overcoming Fear, Worry, and Panic (A New Harbinger Self-Help Workbook) by Matthew McKay, Michelle Skeen, and Patrick Fanning (2017)

The OCD Workbook: Your Guide to Breaking Free from Obsessive-Compulsive Disorder (A New Harbinger Self-Help Workbook) by Bruce M. Hyman and Cherlene Pedrick (2010)

The Anxiety and Worry Workbook: The Cognitive Behavioral Solution by David A. Clark and Aaron T. Beck (2011)

The ACT Workbook for OCD: Mindfulness, Acceptance, and Exposure Skills to Live Well with Obsessive-Compulsive Disorder by Marisa T. Mazza (2020)

Get Out of Your Mind and Into Your Life: The New Acceptance and Commitment Therapy (A New Harbinger Self-Help Workbook) by Steven C. Hayes and Spencer Smith (2005)

Resources for Additional Information, Online Communities, and Support Groups

Anxiety and Depression Association of America: ADAA.org

International OCD Foundation: IOCDF.org

Made of Millions Foundation: Mental Health Advocacy & Education: MadeofMillions.com

Made of Millions online support group for ITs: Facebook.com /groups/intrusivethoughts

CRISIS SUPPORT
National Suicide Prevention Lifeline
SuicidePreventionLifeline.org
1-800-273-8255

Crisis Text Line
CrisisTextLine.org
US and Canada: text 741741
UK: text 85258 | Ireland: text 50808

References

Abramovitch, Amitai, and Avraham Schweiger. "Unwanted Intrusive and Worrisome Thoughts in Adults with Attention Deficit/ Hyperactivity Disorder." *Psychiatry Research* 168, no. 3 (August 2009): 230–233. doi.org/10.1016/j.psychres.2008.06.004.

Anxiety and Depression Association of America. "Facts & Statistics." Accessed July 2020. ADAA.org/about-adaa/press-room /facts-statistics.

Bluett, Ellen J., Kendra J. Homan, Kate L. Morrison, Michael E. Levin, and Michael P. Twohig. "Acceptance and Commitment Therapy for Anxiety and OCD Spectrum Disorders: An Empirical Review." *Journal of Anxiety Disorders* 28, no. 6 (August 2014): 612–624. doi.org/10.1016/j.janxdis.2014.06.008.

Borkovec, T. D., Elwood Robinson, Thomas Pruzinsky, and James A. DePree. "Preliminary Exploration of Worry: Some Characteristics and Processes." *Behavior Research and Therapy* 21, no. 1 (1983): 9–16. doi.org/10.1016/0005-7967(83)90121-3.

Eifert, Georg H., and John P. Forsyth. *Acceptance and Commitment Therapy for Anxiety Disorders: A Practitioner's Treatment Guide to Using Mindfulness, Acceptance, and Values-Based Behavior Change.* Oakland, CA: New Harbinger Publications, 2005.

Geller, Daniel A., and John March. "Practice Parameters for the Assessment and Treatment of Children and Adolescents with Obsessive-Compulsive Disorder." *Journal of the American Academy of Child & Adolescent Psychiatry* 51, no. 1 (January 2012): 98–113. doi.org/10.1016/j.jaac.2011.09.019.

Halliburton, Amanda E., and Lee D. Cooper. "Applications and Adaptations of Acceptance and Commitment Therapy (ACT) for Adolescents." *Journal of Contextual Behavioral Science* 4, no. 1 (January 2015): 1–11. doi.org/10.1016/j.jcbs.2015.01.002.

Hanstede, Marijke, Yori Gidron, and Ivan Nyklíček. "The Effects of a Mindfulness Intervention on Obsessive-Compulsive Symptoms in a Non-Clinical Student Population." *The Journal of Nervous and Mental Disease* 196, no. 10 (October 2008): 776–779. doi.org/10.1097/NMD.0b013e31818786b8.

Hofmann, Stefan G., Alice T. Sawyer, Ashley A. Witt, and Diana Oh. "The Effect of Mindfulness-Based Therapy on Anxiety and Depression: A Meta-Analytic Review." *Journal of Consulting and Clinical Psychology* 78, no. 2 (April 2010): 169–183. doi.org/10.1037/a0018555.

Kissen, Debra, Bari Goldman Cohen, and Kathi Fine Abitbol. *The Panic Workbook for Teens: Breaking the Cycle of Fear, Worry, and Panic Attacks*. Oakland: New Harbinger Publications, 2015.

Kissen, Debra. "Harm-Related OCD." The Huffington Post. Last modified April 16, 2015. HuffPost.com/entry/harm-related -ocdthe-terro_b_6648582.

Ko, Jean Y., Karilynn M. Rockhill, Van T. Tong, Brian Morrow, and Sherry L. Farr. "Trends in Postpartum Depressive Symptoms—27 States, 2004, 2008, and 2012." *Morbidity and Mortality Weekly Report* 66, no. 6 (February 2017): 153–158. dx.doi.org /10.15585/mmwr.mm6606a1.

Koran, Lorrin, Gregory Hanna, Eric Hollander, Gerald Nestadt, and Helen Blair Simpson. "Practice Guideline for the Treatment of Patients with Obsessive-Compulsive Disorder." *The American Journal of Psychiatry* 164, (2007): 5–53.

Law, Clare, and Christina L. Boisseau. "Exposure and Response Prevention in the Treatment of Obsessive-Compulsive Disorder: Current Perspectives." *Psychology Research and Behavior Management* 12, no. 1 (January 2019): 1167–1174. doi.org/10.2147 /PRBM.S211117.

Lipari, Rachel N., and Struther L. Van Horn. "Trends in Substance Use Disorders Among Adults Aged 18 or Older." The Substance Abuse and Mental Health Services Administration (June 2017). SAMHSA.gov/data/sites/default/files/report_2790/ShortReport -2790.html.

Merriam-Webster. "Accept." Accessed July 27, 2020. Merriam-Webster.com/dictionary/accept.

Moulding, Richard, Meredith E. Coles, Jonathan S. Abramowitz, Gillian M. Alcolado, Pino Alonso, Amparo Belloch, Martine Bouvard, David A. Clark, Guy Doron, Héctor Fernández-Álvarez, et al. "Part 2. They Scare Because We Care: The Relationship Between Obsessive Intrusive Thoughts and Appraisals and Control Strategies Across 15 Cities." *Journal of Obsessive-Compulsive and Related Disorders* 3, no. 3 (July 2014): 280–291. doi.org/10.1016 /j.jocrd.2014.02.006.

National Institute of Mental Health. "Attention-Deficit/Hyperactivity Disorder (ADHD)." Last modified November 2017. NIMH.nih.gov /health/statistics/attention-deficit-hyperactivity-disorder-adhd .shtml#part_154905.

National Institute of Mental Health. "Bipolar Disorder." Last modified November 2017. NIMH.nih.gov/health/topics /bipolar-disorder/index.shtml.

National Institute of Mental Health. "Obsessive-Compulsive Disorder (OCD)." Last modified November 2017. NIMH.nih.gov /health/statistics/obsessive-compulsive-disorder-ocd.shtml.

Radomsky, Adam, Gillian Alcolado, Jonathan Abramowitz, Pino Alonso, Amparo Belloch, Martine Bouvard, David Clark, Meredith Coles, Guy Doron, Héctor Fernández-Alvarez, et al. "Part 1—You Can Run but You Can't Hide: Intrusive Thoughts on Six Continents." *Journal of Obsessive-Compulsive and Related Disorders* 3, no. 3 (July 2014): 269–279. doi.org/10.1016/j.jocrd .2013.09.002.

Shikatani, Bethany, Matilda E. Nowakowski, and Martin M. Antony. "Illness Anxiety Disorder/Hypochondriasis." *The Encyclopedia of Clinical Psychology* (January 2015): doi.org/10.1002/9781118625392 .wbecp295.

Index

Acknowledgments

I want to first thank my husband, Jonathan Kohn, and my wonderful (most of the time) children, Jordyn, Jakob, Morgan, and Bowie, for granting me the time away from each of you to write this book. Values-based living for me means spending the precious moments of my life with you, having big moments and small moments and everything in between. So know that I try to think long and hard about what other activities fill my life to make sure they matter. And I do believe writing this book matters. The pain and suffering experienced by those struggling with intrusive thoughts is unnecessary and can be easily eradicated with a bit of psychoeducation and compassionate coaching; I hope this is exactly what this book provides to you, the reader. I want to thank the countless individuals who have reached out to me to share their stories of wrestling with intrusive thoughts. You inspire me with your honesty and bravery and overall goodness. You strive so ardently to be good that you never give yourself a break. This book is for you. I am hoping that upon reading it you will provide yourself with additional self-compassion and understand that living a good life is about what you do and not what you think.

I also want to thank my wonderful Light on Anxiety staff. Each of you put your heart and soul into helping those struggling with anxiety and related behavioral health challenges to live their best lives. I feel blessed to know each of you. I hope each of you know the difference you are making in this world with all of your dedication and hard work. And specifically, to my utterly fabulous coauthors, Dr. Micah Ioffe and Emily Lambert. I could not imagine a smoother writing project and that is because we work so well together. This has been a true team experience, with easy, fluid handoffs. I am thrilled that we had this opportunity to work together and write this important book.

And finally, to my dad, Judy, Suzi, and Nathalie, you are and have always been my cheering section and I can't imagine what I would do without your unconditional love and support.

With deep appreciation,
Debra Kissen, PhD, MHSA

I would first like to extend a very heartfelt thank-you to my family—my "day one supporters." To my parents, Yana and Dave, for their sacrifices, wise counsel, and loving support. To Baba and Zeida, who have been my dearest role models in everything I've pursued: Thank you for your constant love, encouragement, and a sympathetic ear. To my sister, Daryn, for constantly challenging me to reach my full potential both as a person and as a psychologist. I look up to each and every one of you and am lucky to have you by my side every step of the way.

To Aaron and Tito: Thank you for your uplifting presence and always cheering me on. You challenge me in meaningful ways and encourage me to live my best life. There is no one else I would rather be at home with (and while writing a book) during a pandemic, and I'm immensely grateful for both of you.

Thank you to my lovely coauthors: I am so appreciative of our team efforts, playful approach, and collective wisdom. This has been such a fun and rewarding experience with both of you.

Thank you to my mentors throughout the years for all your guidance, teachings, and inspiration, all of which have equipped me to help others through their struggles in many ways, including through this book.

And a sincere thank-you and appreciation to my clients: You continue to inspire me to step outside my comfort zone and wow me with your willingness and bravery each and every time you break free from your fears.

With gratitude,
Micah Ioffe, PhD

First and foremost, I extend my deepest gratitude to my coauthors, Dr. Debra Kissen and Dr. Micah Ioffe. Thank you for allowing me to be part of this fast-paced journey with you. It was with awe that I watched your wisdom and creativity flourish week after week.

To my incredible parents, Rob and Karen: Thank you for supporting my curiosities and endeavors. It has been through your example that I've learned how to use both my brain and my heart. And Brian, brother, thank you for offering an escape into your world across the pond.

I couldn't have participated in this project without Andrew, who provided me with love and encouragement that often kept me steadied, afloat, and fed. Thank you for loving me no matter what.

Thank you to my friends, Erin, Justine, and Maggie, who will always be intimately intertwined in this chapter of my life. Your collective fortitude has been an unyielding power source.

And finally, to my clients: Every day I am in awe of your bravery to show up and do hard things. I am honored to journey alongside each of you. Know that I see you for the whole, wise beings that you are and always have been. It is my hope that this book can help guide you to seeing and experiencing yourselves in that way.

With gratitude,
Emily Lambert, LPC, NCC

About the Authors

 Debra Kissen, PhD, MHSA, is CEO of Light on Anxiety CBT Treatment Center. Dr. Kissen specializes in cognitive behavioral therapy (CBT) for anxiety and related disorders. Dr. Kissen is the author of the *Panic Workbook for Teens* and *Rewire Your Anxious Brains for Teens: Using CBT, Neuroscience, and Mindfulness to Help You End Anxiety, Panic, and Worry (The Instant Help Solutions Series)* and shares information on empirically supported treatment for anxiety and related disorders. Dr. Kissen also has a special interest in the principles of mindfulness and their application for anxiety disorders. Dr. Kissen has presented her research on CBT and mindfulness-based treatments for anxiety and related disorders at regional and national conferences.

 Micah Ioffe, PhD, is a licensed clinical psychologist who specializes in the treatment of anxiety disorders. She earned her PhD in Clinical Psychology from Northern Illinois University. Dr. Ioffe is coauthor of *Rewire Your Anxious Brains for Teens: Using CBT, Neuroscience, and Mindfulness to Help You End Anxiety, Panic, and Worry (The Instant Help Solutions Series)* and has authored multiple research publications. Dr. Ioffe utilizes both cognitive behavioral therapy (CBT) and acceptance and commitment therapy (ACT) in her work with clients to help them move through anxious moments feeling empowered, fulfilled, and brave.

Emily Lambert, LPC, NCC, is a clinical mental health counselor at Light on Anxiety CBT Treatment Center. Emily received her Master of Arts in Counseling from Northwestern University. Emily uses a foundation of cognitive behavioral therapy (CBT) and a humanistic perspective to help clients harness their innate strengths and address unhelpful, self-defeating thoughts and behavioral patterns to learn to work, love, and play more vibrantly and effectively.